AF262924

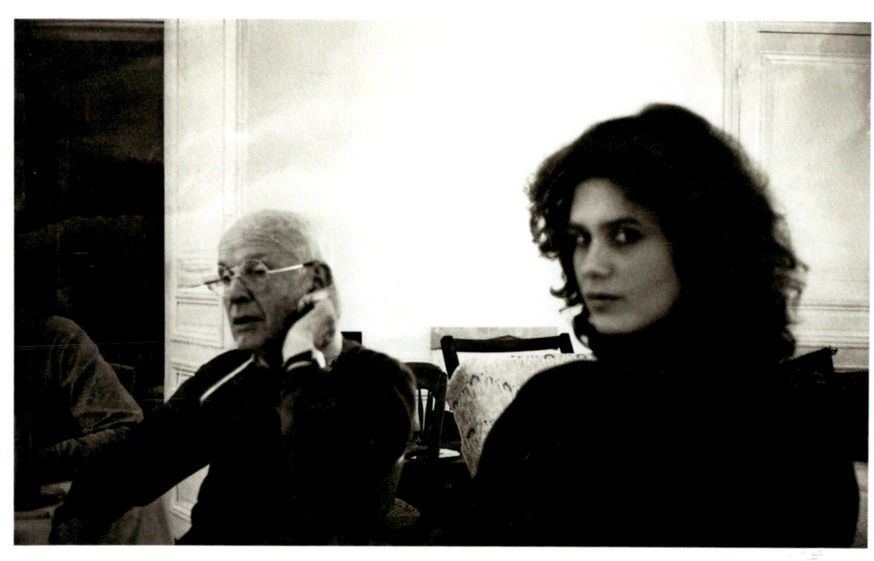

Henri Cartier-Bresson and Anne Day, Paris, by Hervé Guibert, 1981

Anne Day

les floshe d'Anne

Magic Hour Press
2025

EDITOR'S NOTE

In 2024, I was working on the publication of *Suzanne and Louise* by the French photographer and writer Hervé Guibert. A friend and colleague, Elizabeth Gaffin, was at a dinner party at Anne Day's house in Salisbury, Connecticut, and mentioned that forthcoming book. To her surprise, Anne remarked simply, referring to Guibert: "I knew him, you know, in the early 80s. We were good friends." This book is the dreamlike, uncanny result of that serendipitous encounter with a remarkable woman.

—Jordan Weitzman

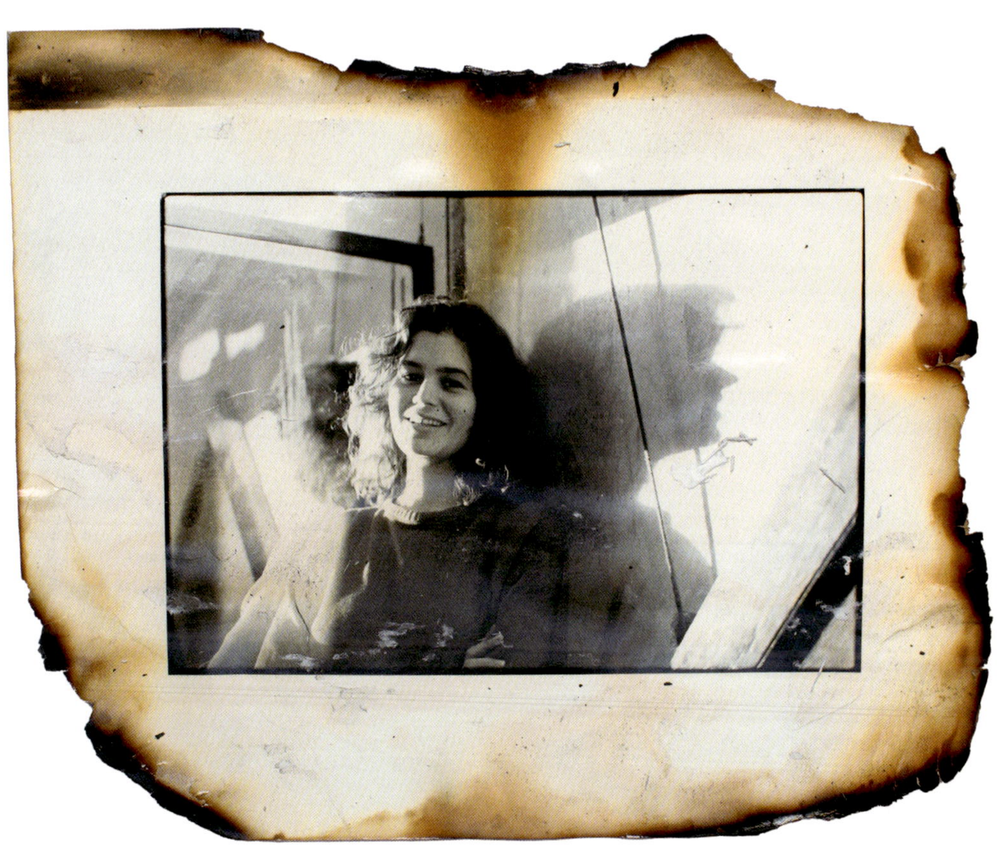

Self-portrait, New York City, 1981

You know, I never really planned for any of it. It was like, I was walking down the street and there was Orson. Okay, not exactly like that, but things just happened to me. I met all of these interesting people…

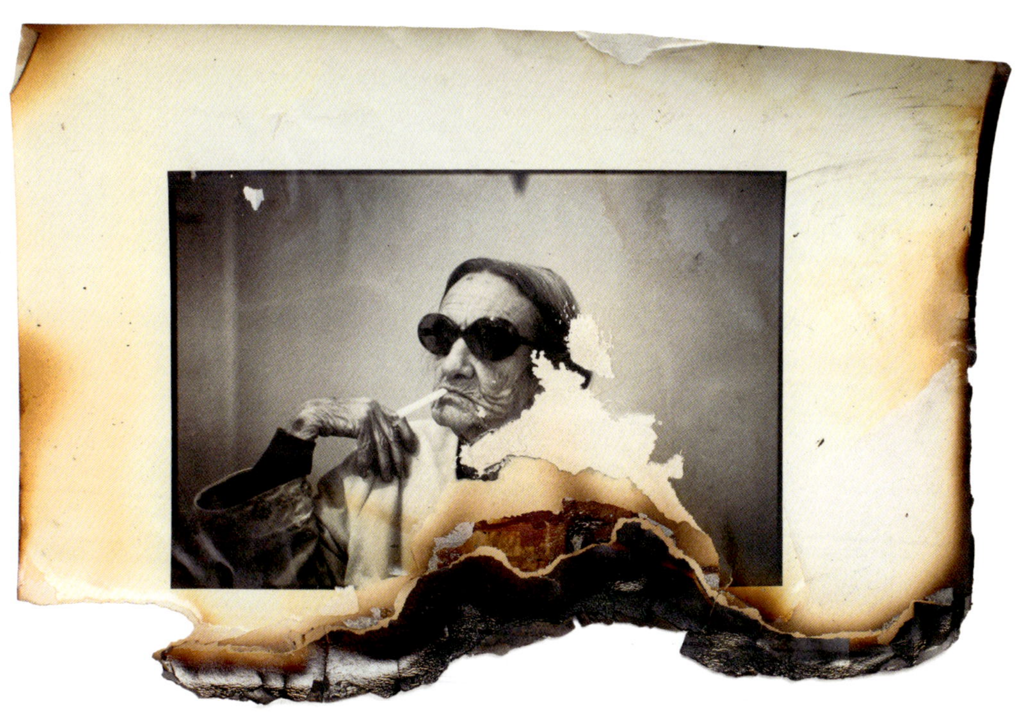

Grandma, Washington, DC, 1977

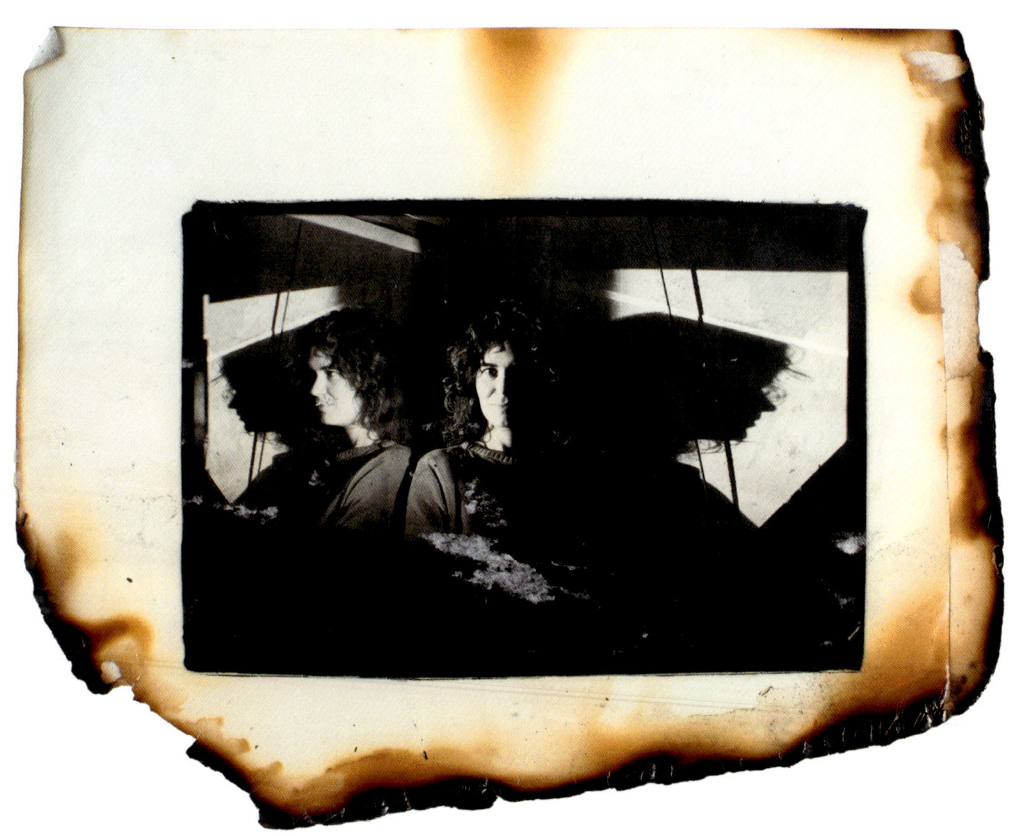

Self-portrait, New York City, 1981

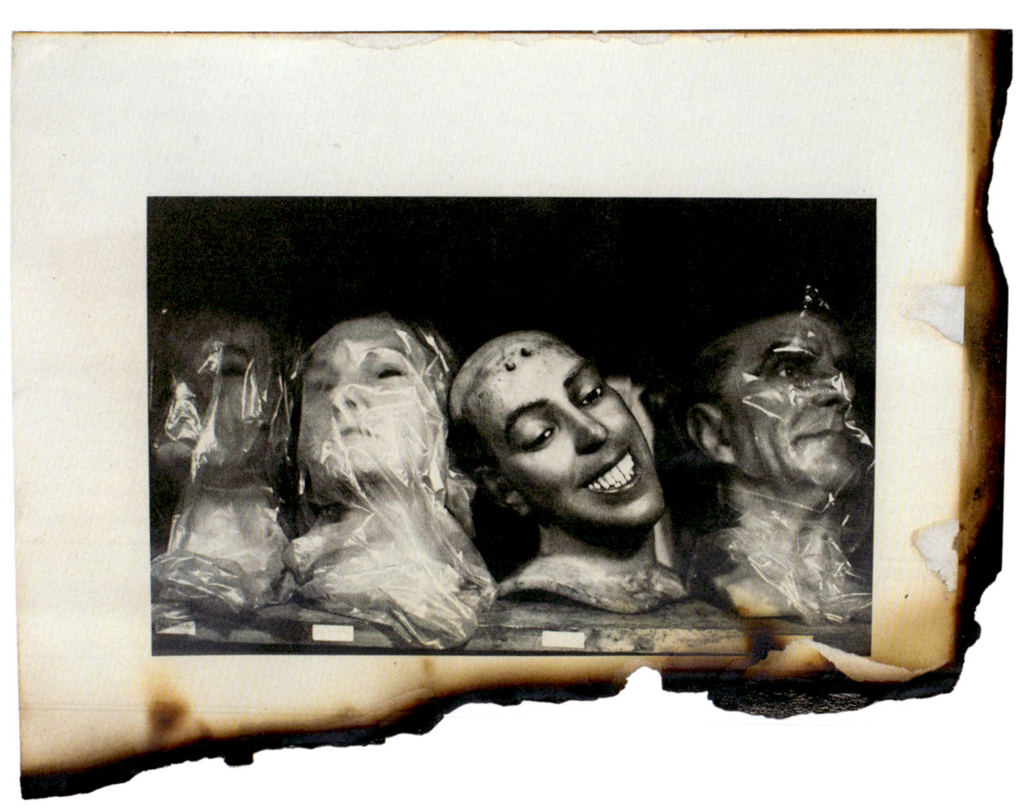

Musée Grévin, Paris, 1981

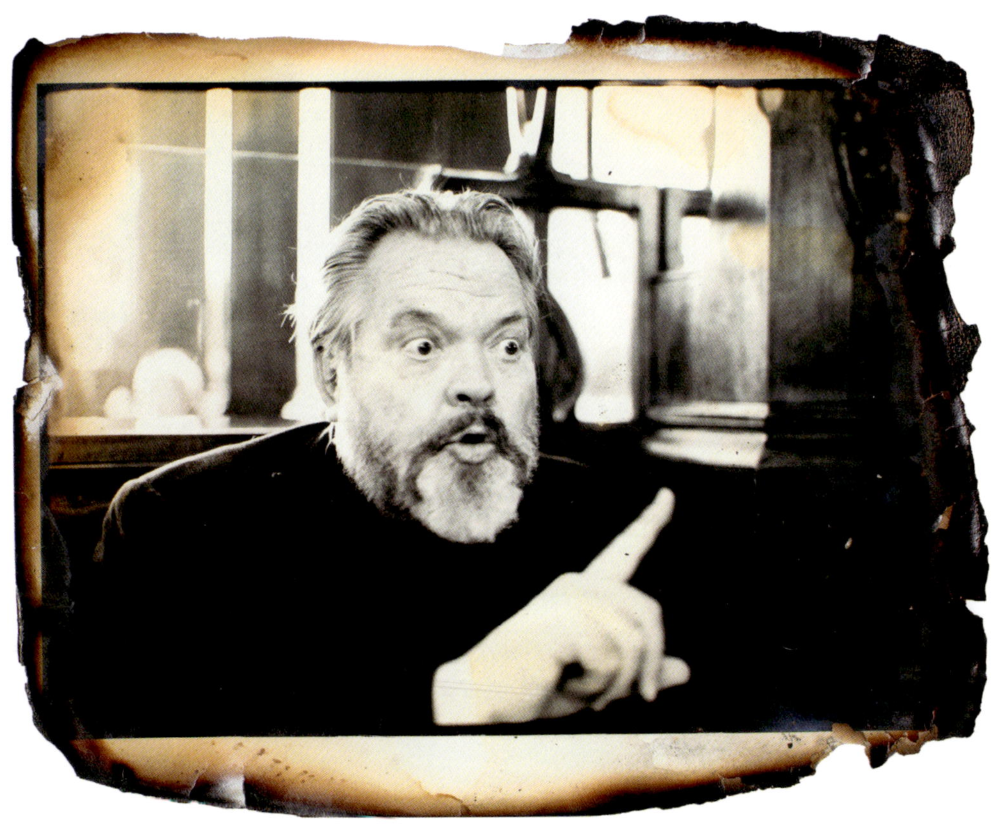

Orson Welles, Paris, 1982

After the fire happened, every time I'd
look in the rubble, I'd see an Orson photo
floating up from the ash.

You'll see, I don't really remember that much.

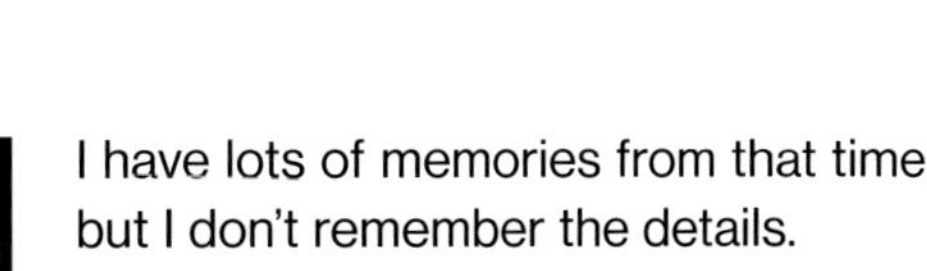

I have lots of memories from that time,
but I don't remember the details.

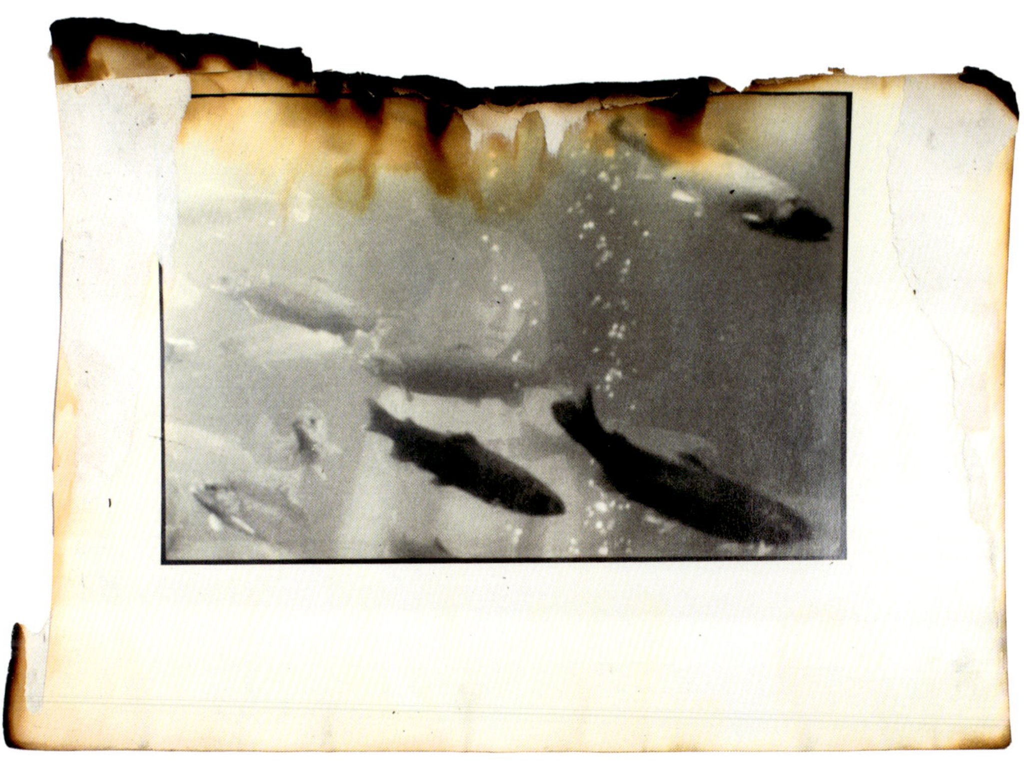

Isabelle Huppert, Besançon, France, 1982

Versailles, France, 1982

What I do remember is that Hervé really loved my photographs of my grandmother. He thought they were so extraordinary. He had just published *Suzanne and Louise*. He said, "Why are you wasting your time doing these dumb jobs?" And I thought, "Well, if you'd like to pay my rent…" I didn't say that, but I did have to make a living, and I wasn't making a living photographing my grandmother.

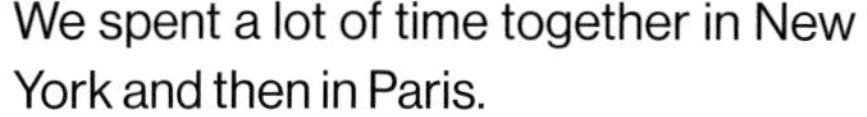
We spent a lot of time together in New
York and then in Paris.

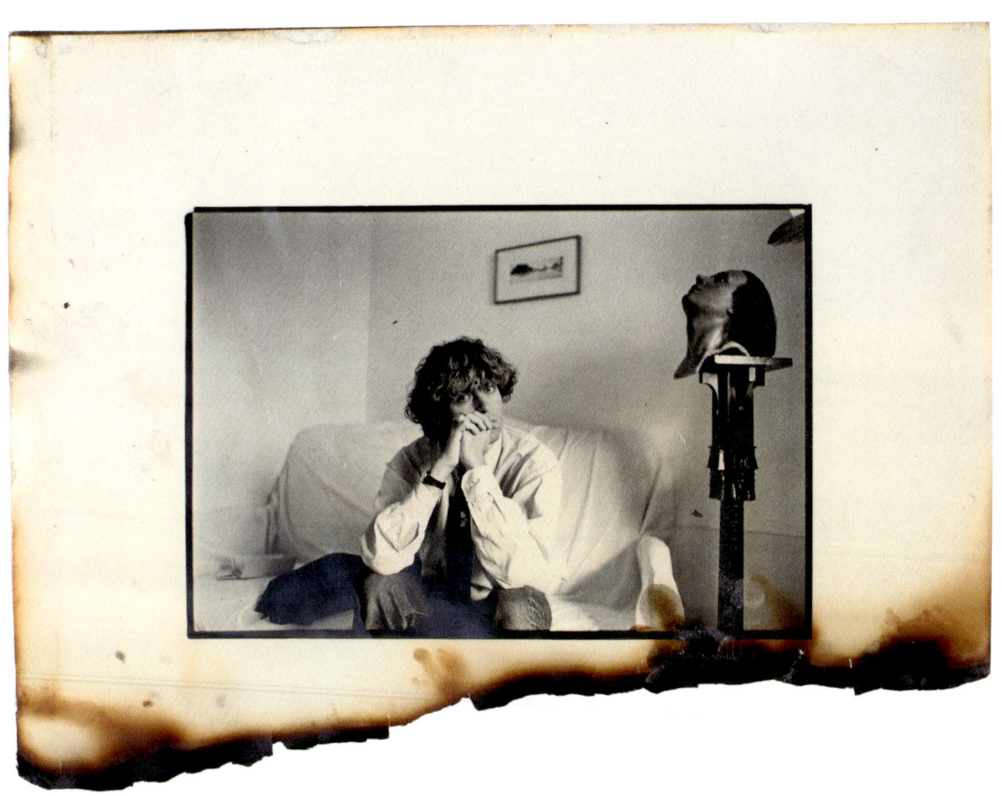

Hervé Guibert, Paris, 1981

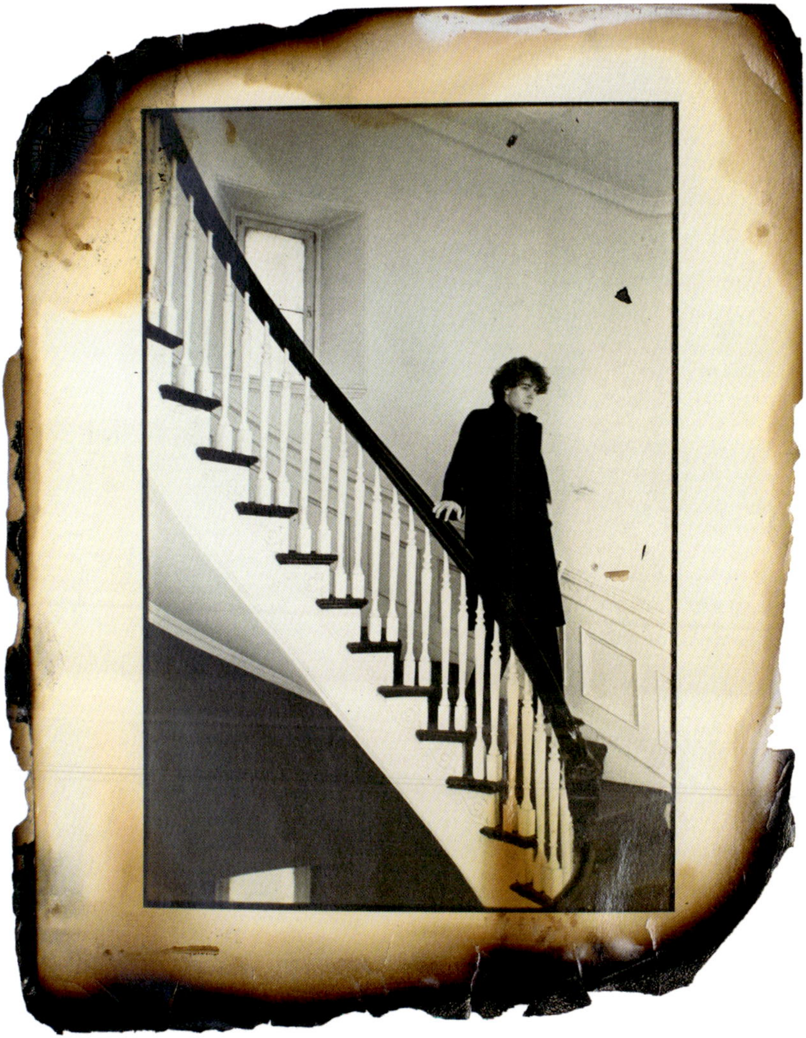

Hervé Guibert, Paris, 1981

Before Hervé, at a dinner in New York back in 1980, I met these French people, Yvonne and Roger. They were friends of Buddy, the friend who brought me, who was trying to unload a large quantity of blue jeans and they were interested in buying Buddy's house in Spetses, Greece. (As it turned out, nobody got what they wanted.) Yvonne was the cultural editor of *Le Monde*, and Roger was a writer from the US who had lived in Paris for a long time. Such a long story. They took a liking to me, and then, the next time they came, they invited me to dinner with Daniel Toscan du Plantier and Isabelle Huppert.

Toscan du Plantier was the director-general of Gaumont. I'm pretty sure he's the one who discovered Isabelle Huppert. He had also produced every great film you've ever seen that was made in France between like 1970 and 2000 or something. He had been married to the actress Marie Christine Barrault, whom I adored from that movie *Cousin Cousine.*

Toscan du Plantier was seemingly single and they were trying to fix me up with him. But it turned out he was Isabelle's boyfriend, or something resembling that. He was certainly her champion. At some point that summer, they arranged a dinner with me that did not include Isabelle. I did not know this Toscan du Plantier (called "Toscan" by the cognoscenti), but he said that he wanted to marry me. I was bewildered — I remember thinking: *This is so fucking weird. He doesn't know me, he's never even kissed me, but he thinks he wants to marry me?* French people are so odd.

At that dinner, he showed me a picture of his house in the South of France. I remember it was a lovely pink color with white shutters on the windows. The house was very plain, elegant, large and old. Touching the photograph of one of the shuttered windows, he said, "That's my room." Pointing to another window, he said, "That can be your room." And I said, "Wait, we won't be sleeping in the same room?" He said, "Oh, we can if you want."

The morning after that embarrassing proposal, a letter was delivered to me by messenger at my apartment. It was on thick Gaumont stationery, handwritten, three pages. I might have forgotten this detail, but I found the letter in the fire remains. He kind of re-did the marriage proposal and also apologized. He wrote something to the tune of, "I'm really sorry. I know that was really embarrassing for you. We should get to know each other," da, da, da.

And I felt like… you know what I felt like? I said it to them at the time. I said, "It's like I'm a horse on a trading block. And you all are saying, 'Oh, she is this, she is that. She'd be perfect for you. Oh, she's got…" And somehow I was supposed to be interested because he was a big deal. I suppose I was willing to check it out, but it was odd. It was like that. I was pretty young. I think I was 26, whatever I was, I was 25, maybe. I don't remember. None of it felt right, but at the time I could not exactly say why.

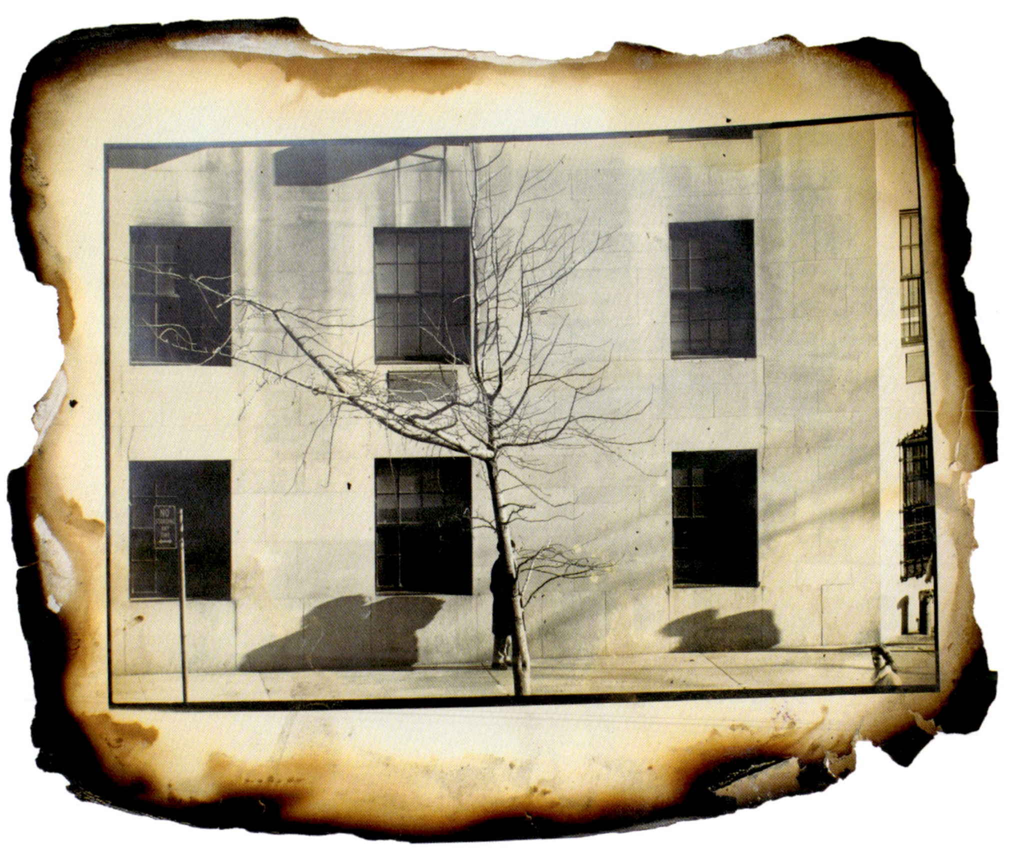

One 5th Avenue, New York City, 1981

Then I guess this couple, the *Le Monde* editor and her husband, they might have felt ashamed. I remember I said, "That's kind of gross what you just did, trying to fix me up with this guy based on the way I look, the fact that I'm American." It had nothing to do with me. And I said, "It's kind of insulting." I must have said it nicely; I would have then. And then the wife called me to apologize. And the husband said, "Anyway you must come to Paris and you can stay with us." So eventually, I did.

But before that happened—I mean, before going to Paris, they sent Hervé to me in New York. He was coming because he was doing some interviews for *Le Monde* and he had never been to New York City before. They knew me, I was his age, they thought we would get along. So Roger sent me a note and asked, "Would it be okay if Hervé Guibert comes to stay with you? He's a photo critic, you two will like each other." And I was like, "Yeah, okay, I guess."

I remember it was a cold night, around 10pm, when he showed up at my door. His flight had just gotten in from Paris, and he had this big box of Guerlain perfume. It was wrapped in beautiful pink paper. I've never forgotten that detail. It was a very pale pink, heavy paper, not shiny, almost like a shopping bag paper. The box was tied with a navy blue grosgrain ribbon.* He was solemn and serious at first, and I was like, "Oh, hi!" I'd just gotten out of the shower. Later, he always told the story—'She was like an American movie star, like, Doris Day would open the door, and she'd have a towel wrapped around her head.' And it wasn't on purpose. It's just that he arrived earlier than I thought. So then he came in, and we became friends from that moment, right away. We did everything in New York together. I introduced him to my friends, and we went to galleries, and he took me on his interviews.

*The perfume was a bottle of *Eau du Coq*, a fabulous lemony scent in the signature Guerlain bottle. When I got to know him, I learned that Hervé wore *Habit Rouge*. That scent still reminds me of him.

He interviewed André Kertész, who actually lived in my building, up on a high floor at 2 Fifth Ave. So Hervé brought me to the interview. And he somehow knew that Kertész only drank Lillet. So we bought him a bottle of Lillet and presented it to him.

Hervé had scheduled the interview, but he had no idea that Kertész was in my building, by the way, it was just a total coincidence. Kertész had been doing all those SX-70 Polaroids out of his window, you know, all those pictures overlooking Washington Square Park. I asked him why he was shooting with the Polaroid, and he said that he wasn't sure how long he'd live and he didn't want to wait for the film to get developed. So the SX-70 was perfect. He seemed really old then. That was 1981. He must have been in his 80s. He was one of my photographer heroes, still is.

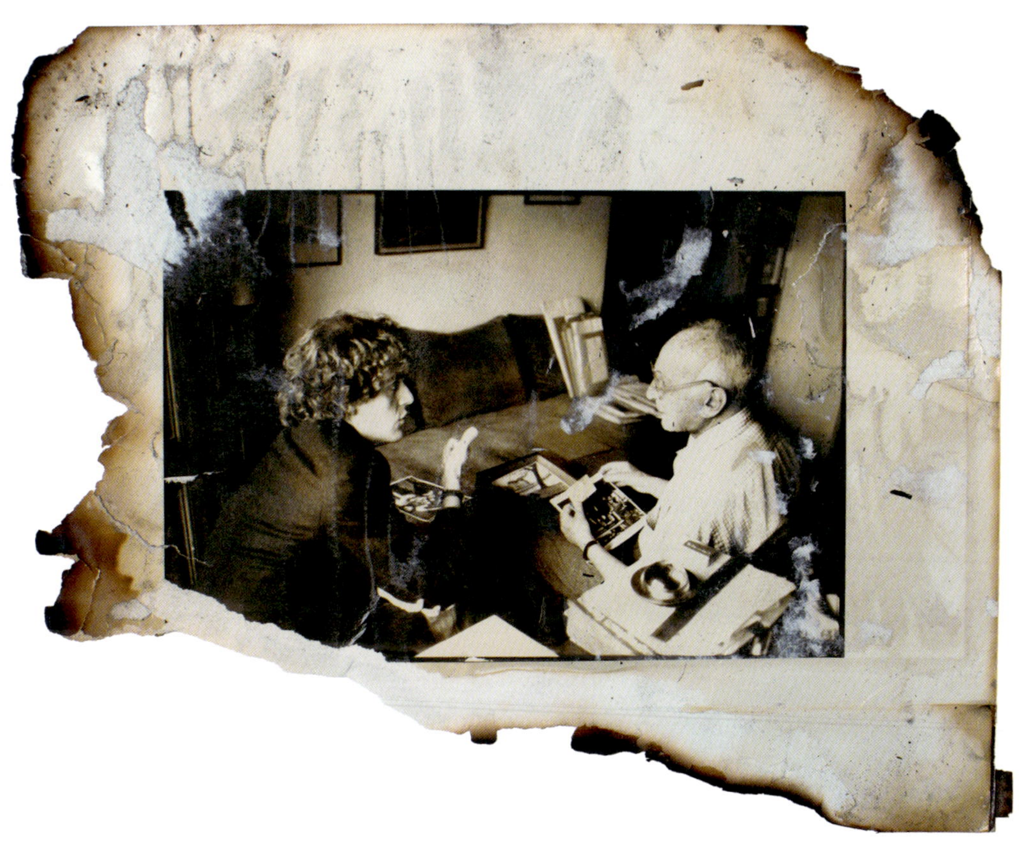

Hervé Guibert and André Kertész, New York City, 1981

Then there was this whole Gina Lollobrigida section of that visit. You know, the Italian movie star from the 1960s. She had a photography show in Rome, and Hervé had written about it, so he knew her.

So when he came to New York, he called her up. And the three of us went to the theater together. Don't ask me what play we saw, because I do not remember. For the life of me, I don't remember. I wish I could. If my notebooks hadn't burned, I would have it because I had all my diaries for every year beginning in 1973. Not a diary like, "Today I ate sushi with Dominique Sanda and she had the uramaki and I had the maguro nigiri"—but a diary like, "4 o'clock dentist appointment." That kind of a diary. And the name of the play would have been in there.

Anyway, I remember it was pouring rain. And it was cold. When he came to visit, it was a cold month, maybe February. We went to Gina Lollobrigida's apartment in the United Nations Plaza, and it was like a hotel suite, nothing personal in the rooms. We had a drink in the living room and then she opened her hall closet to get ready, and there were like nine or ten mink coats in there, all dyed different colors. There was a turquoise, a pink, a white, a black, of course a regular mink coat—brown, yellow. Every color fur was in there. I remembered she tried on the turquoise one but then she chose the natural brown one.

That night, we went to the theater, and then after, we stood out in the rain and there were no cabs. You know what Broadway is like after the theater, there were taxis everywhere, all busy and it was raining. And this police car pulled up and he called, "Gina! Gina!" And he signaled for us to get in and he gave us a ride. He got out and opened the door for Gina, and she sat up front.

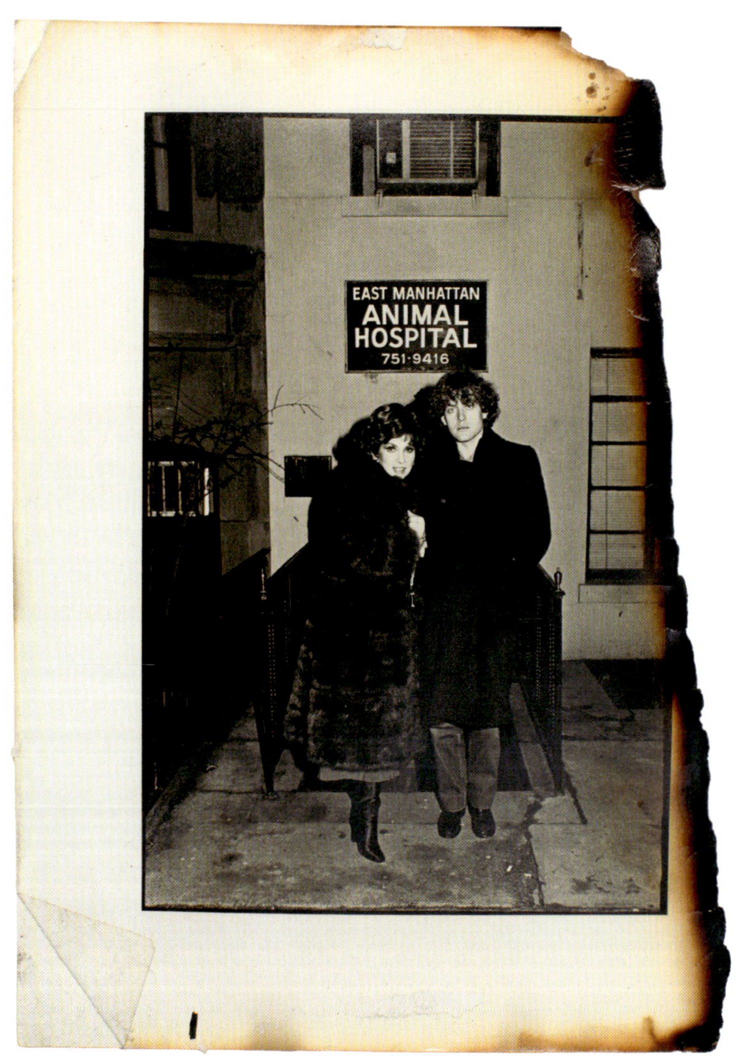

Gina Lollobrigida and Hervé Guibert, New York City, 1981

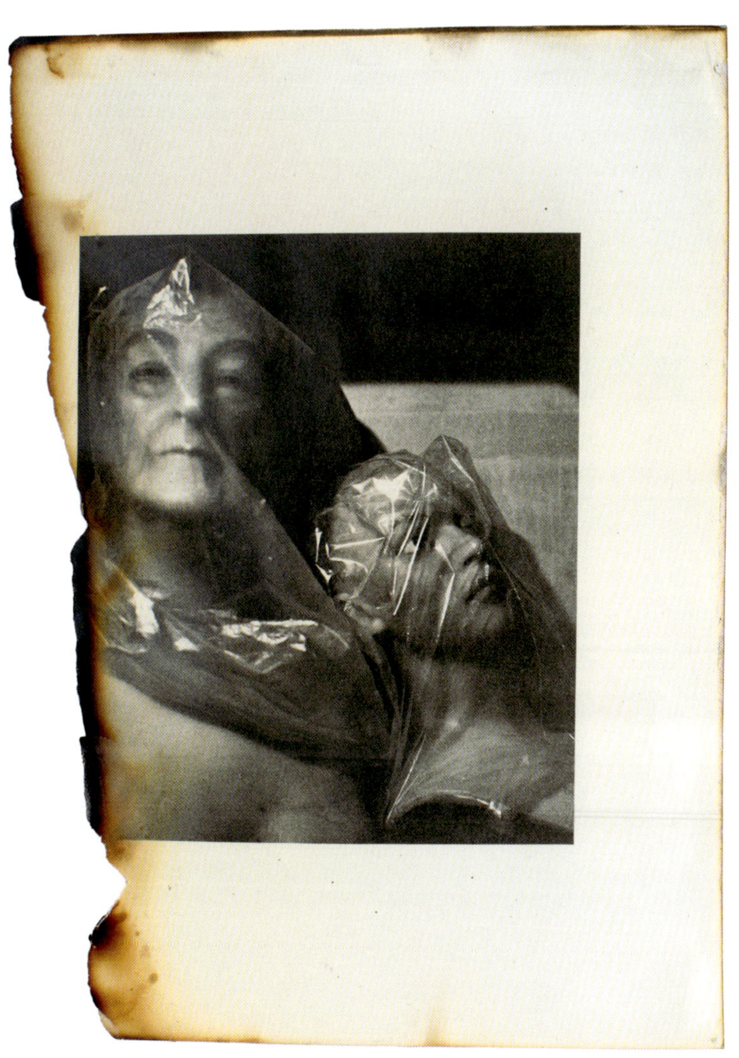

Hervé wrote about it. His details must be better than mine. I just remember thinking, "Well, it's nice but funny to hang around with Gina."

But that was the thing with him. Sometimes I read some of his stories and I wondered whether it was real or if it was just made up for the sake of writing or if it was fantasy on purpose. But then there were things that he wrote about, like this time, where it seemed like a tall tale, but was totally true.

After Hervé left New York, Gina invited me to lunch. She was so lovesick and did not understand why Hervé didn't love her the way she loved him. Other than the 30ish-year age difference, which she did not see as a problem, I suggested that he preferred boys—she was horrified.

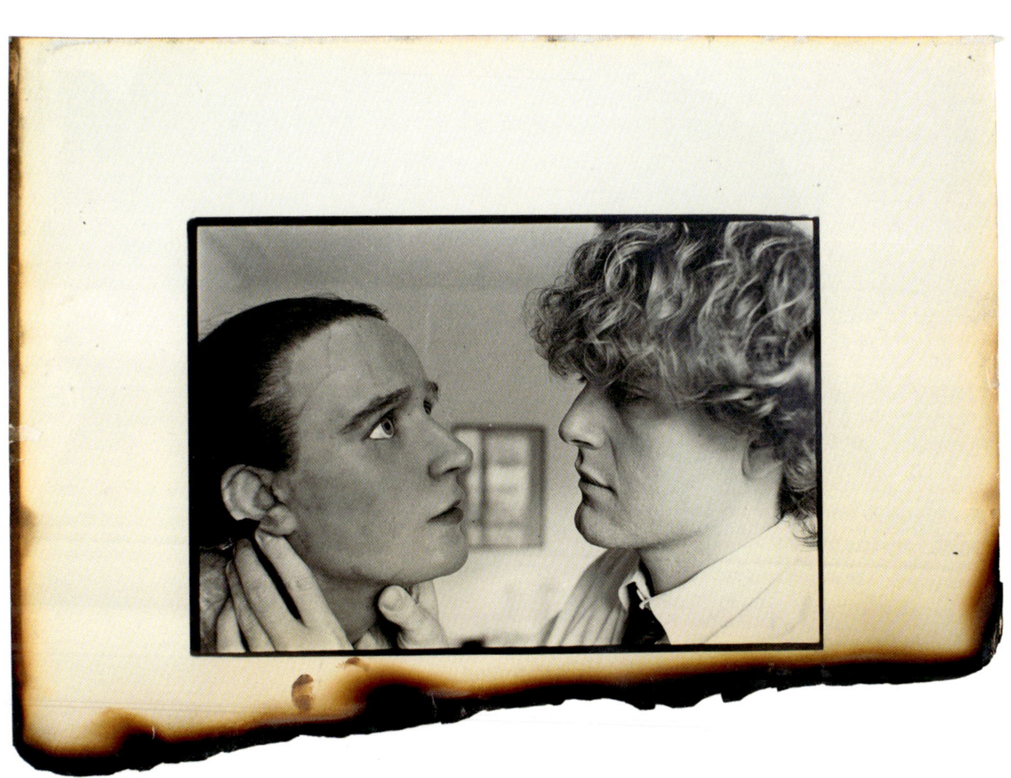

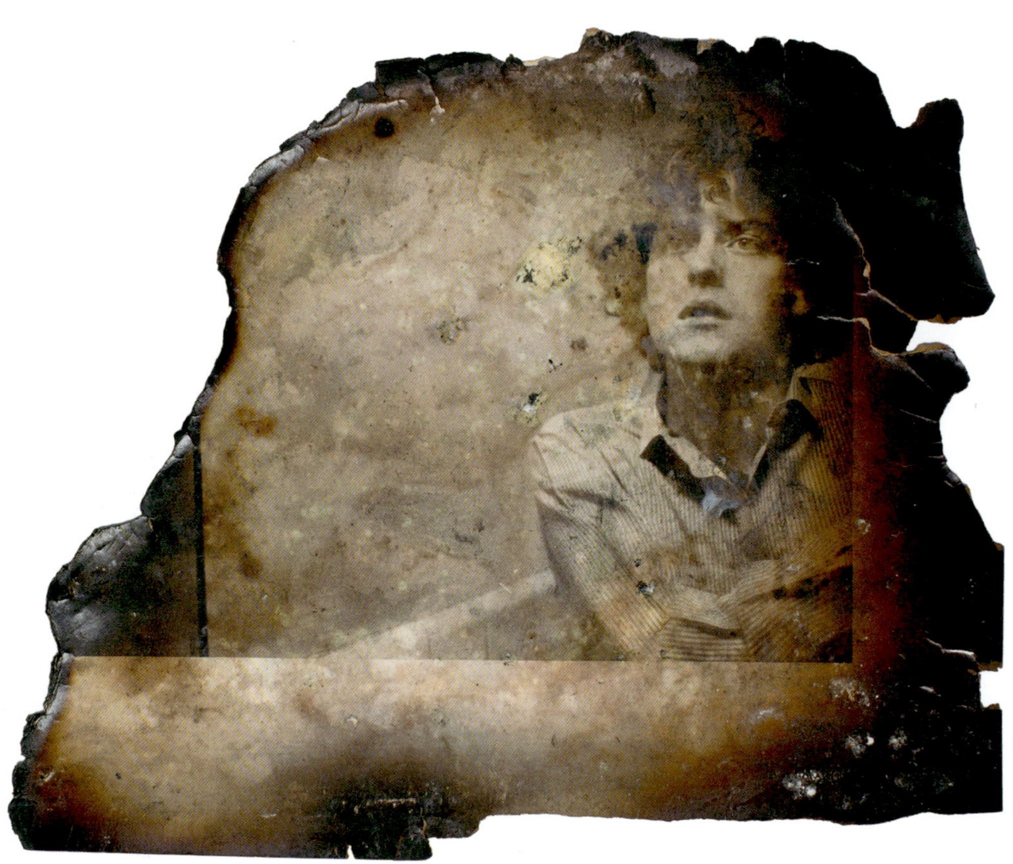

Self-portrait, Hervé Guibert, New York City, 1981

One night in NY, we smoked pot with some of my friends, and Hervé got too stoned; he took a self-portrait in the bathroom mirror in my apartment. Later, he sent me a signed print with a nice note on the back, but I can't even make it out now, it's so burnt.

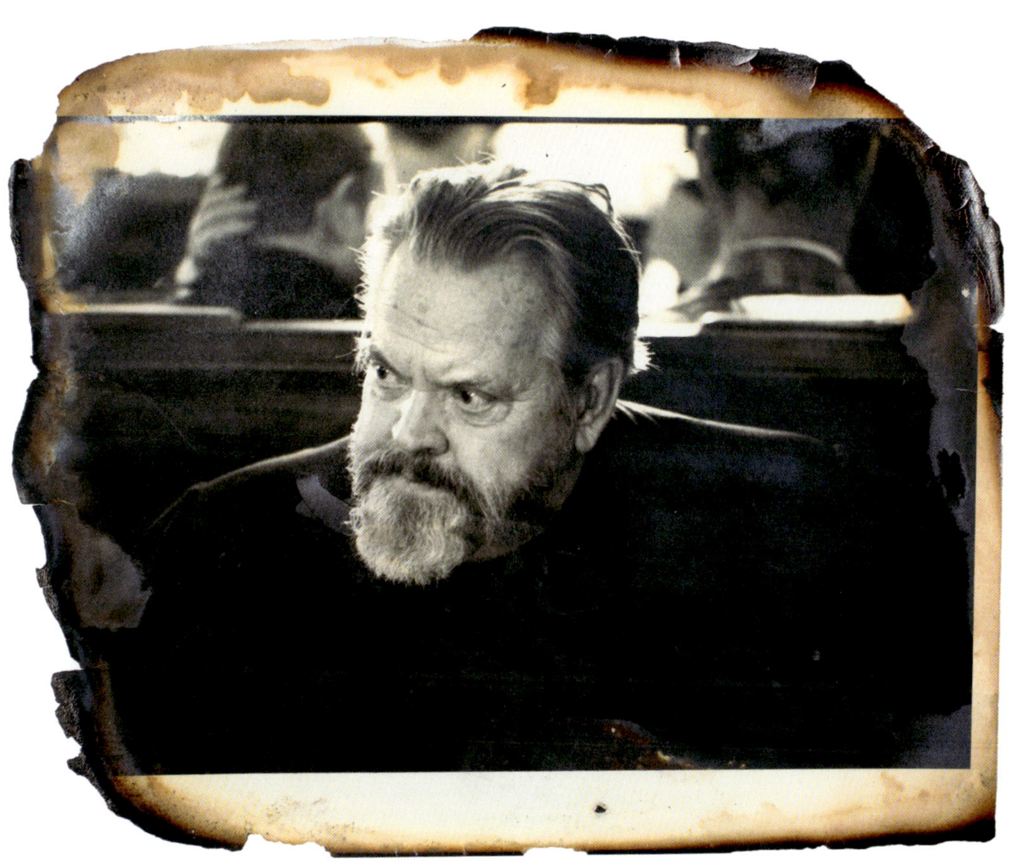

So, okay, here's the story:

Our house burned to the ground in about 10 minutes. At about 4am one cool fall morning in October, 2013, my husband Spencer woke me and told me to get our friend Maria from her room and call 911. I got Maria and we ran until we were in complete blackness. I jumped out a window. Maria was right behind me. But somehow she did not jump out of the window after me — Spencer and I went to all the windows after I hit the ground, and did not see her. I had no phone so I went to a neighbor to get help. By then the house was fully engulfed. As we were driving off to the hospital, I looked up and I saw there was nothing but a skeleton of the house visible through the flames. Maria did not get out.

One little corner of my basement studio where my file cabinets were with my film archives did not totally burn. That was it, the only suggestion of something left from the entire house. So my friend Christopher went and threw a tarp over it because it began to rain that afternoon of the fire.

Later, I found many negatives and prints
from my film days.

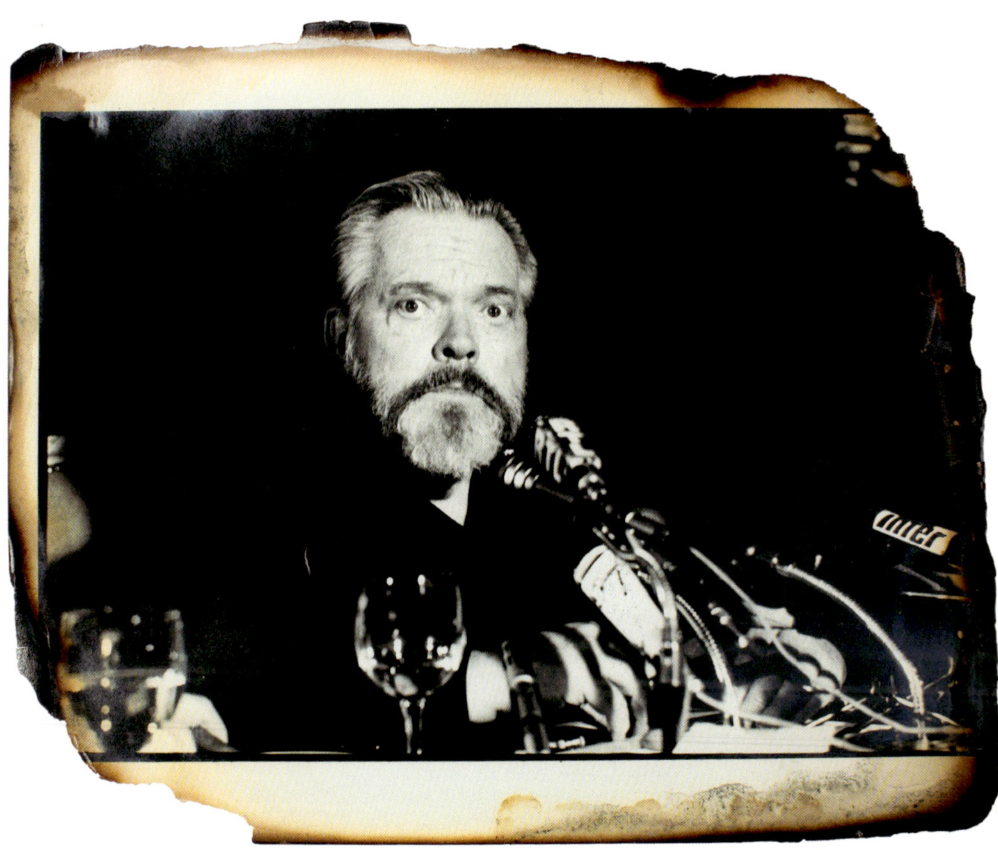

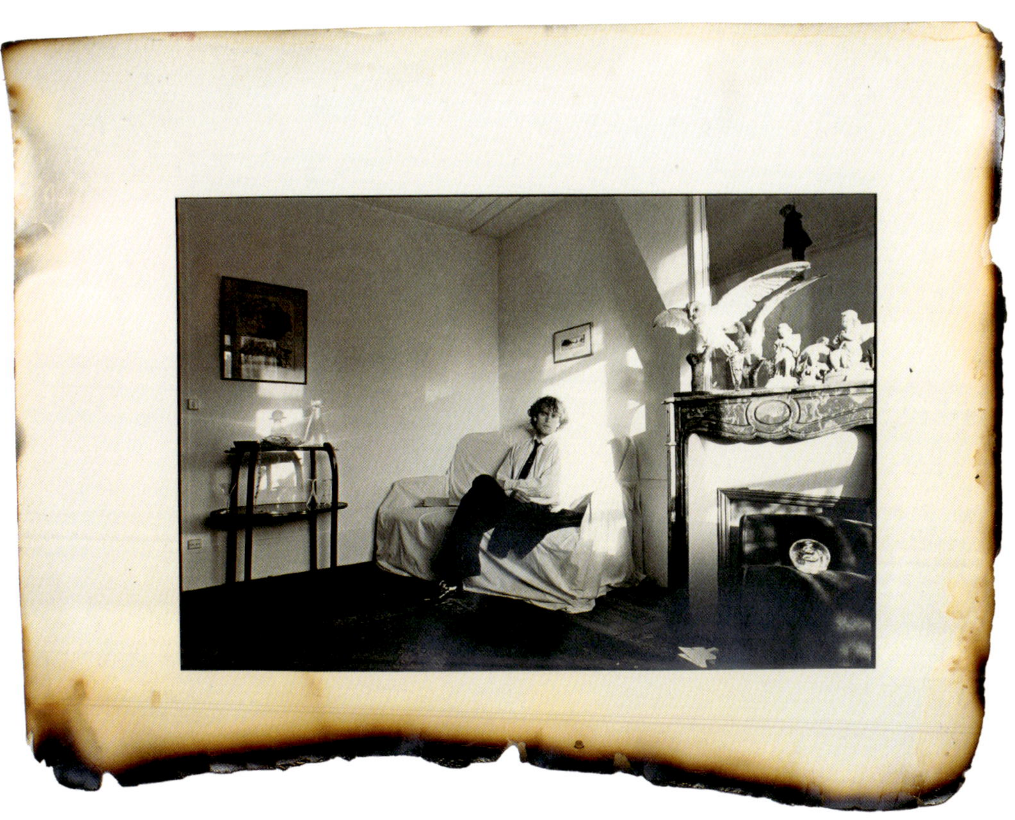

Hervé Guibert in his apartment, Paris, 1981

I moved to Paris in 1981 because I had a job. Toscan du Plantier maybe felt slightly guilty from that time he proposed to me for no real reason, and he offered me a job on one of his movie sets—a Joseph Losey film called *La Truite,* starring Isabelle Huppert. She played a clever girl who grew up on a trout farm and, like the trout, she swims her way up through high society, milking men for all they're worth, the way, as a girl, she milked the trout for their eggs.

I was living in Paris, working on this movie set, and Isabelle befriended me. She once invited me over to the very posh apartment near the Parc Monceau she shared with Toscan. Although the apartment was very elegant, I'm pretty sure Isabelle lived in a back room, almost like a maid's room.

She took me into her bedroom, which was kind of spare, but she had three slide projectors set up. So I sat on her bed, and the three slide projectors pointed at three walls. All had pictures of her. And she wanted me to help her decide which ones she should use for various purposes which I cannot remember.

Anyway, it was awkward. It was a little strange because other people told me that Isabelle thought Toscan was trying to go out with me, but by then, he definitely was not. Eventually, while he was not in Paris, I got fired after about a month on that movie. Everyone said it was Isabelle who made that happen, but I don't know. The men in suits came to me and said, "You know you can't work on this movie because you don't have the right papers." I asked, "Why did you hire me?" And they said, "Well you know, for a short time it's okay, but you are not part of the syndicate." The 'syndicate,' which I guess means the union.

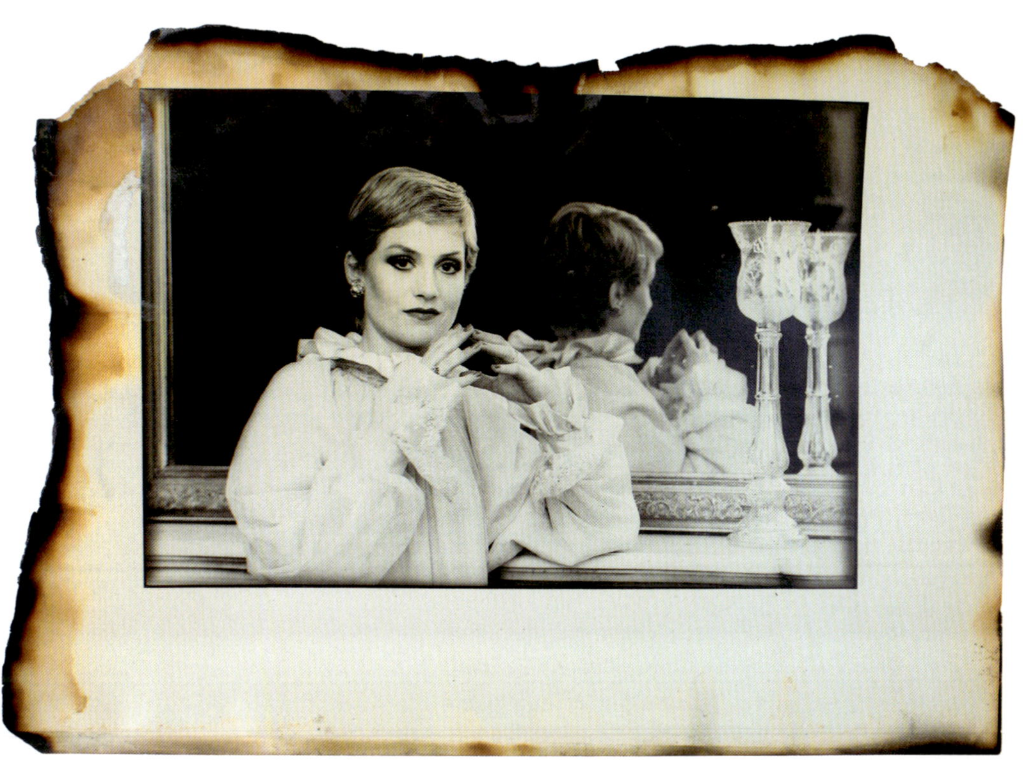

Isabelle Huppert, Paris, 1982

Later, after he heard what happened, Toscan got me put on another movie as the set photographer, which also ended badly. (This time, the line producer, who was the brother of the star, Gerard Depardieu, grabbed me by the ass and I complained to his boss — guess who had to leave the set?) France was like that. I suppose the world was like that in 1982, but I had so little experience. I was so humiliated.

Toscan did get married three times after he proposed to me and his third wife was murdered in Ireland.

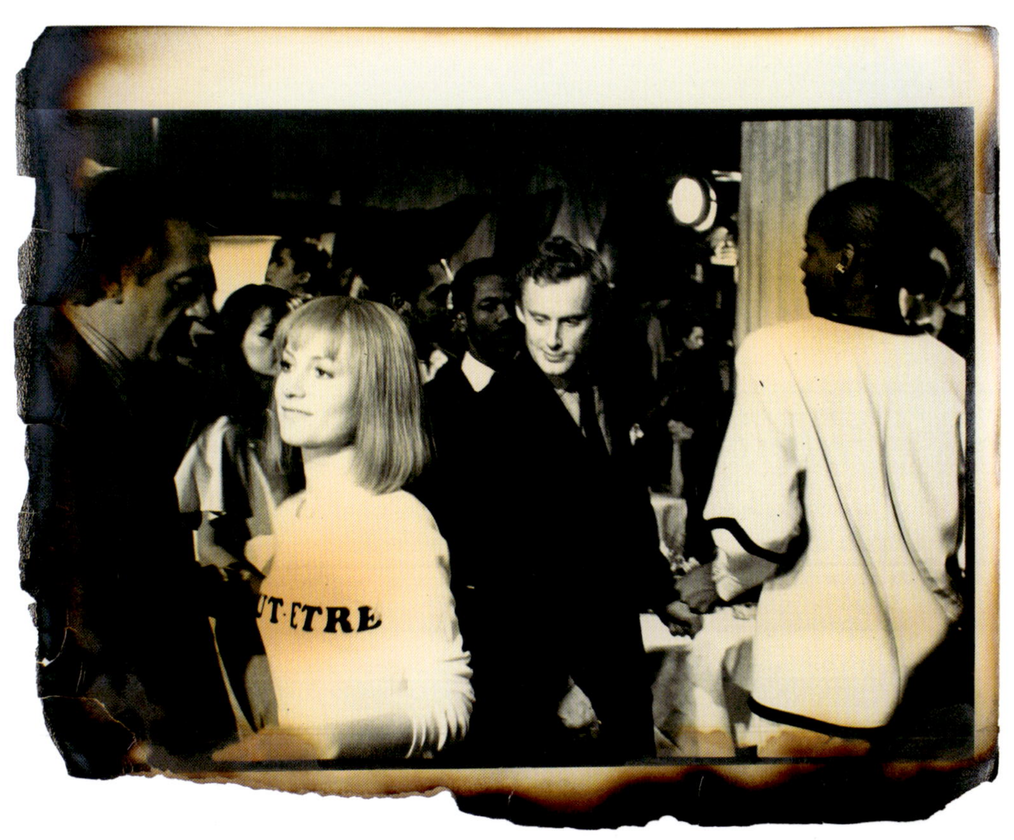

Set of *La Truite* (dir. Joseph Losey), Besançon, France, 1982

In the meantime, I was already in Paris, and I knew Hervé from our time in New York. We went everywhere together. He took me to all the dance performances because he was also the dance critic for *Le Monde*. He took me to Mark Morris and Pina Bausch—that whole movement in modern dance in the 80s was so revolutionary. And we went to galleries together and we'd go out to dinner. We hung out with Thierry and Christine, his best friends and the love of Hervé's life.

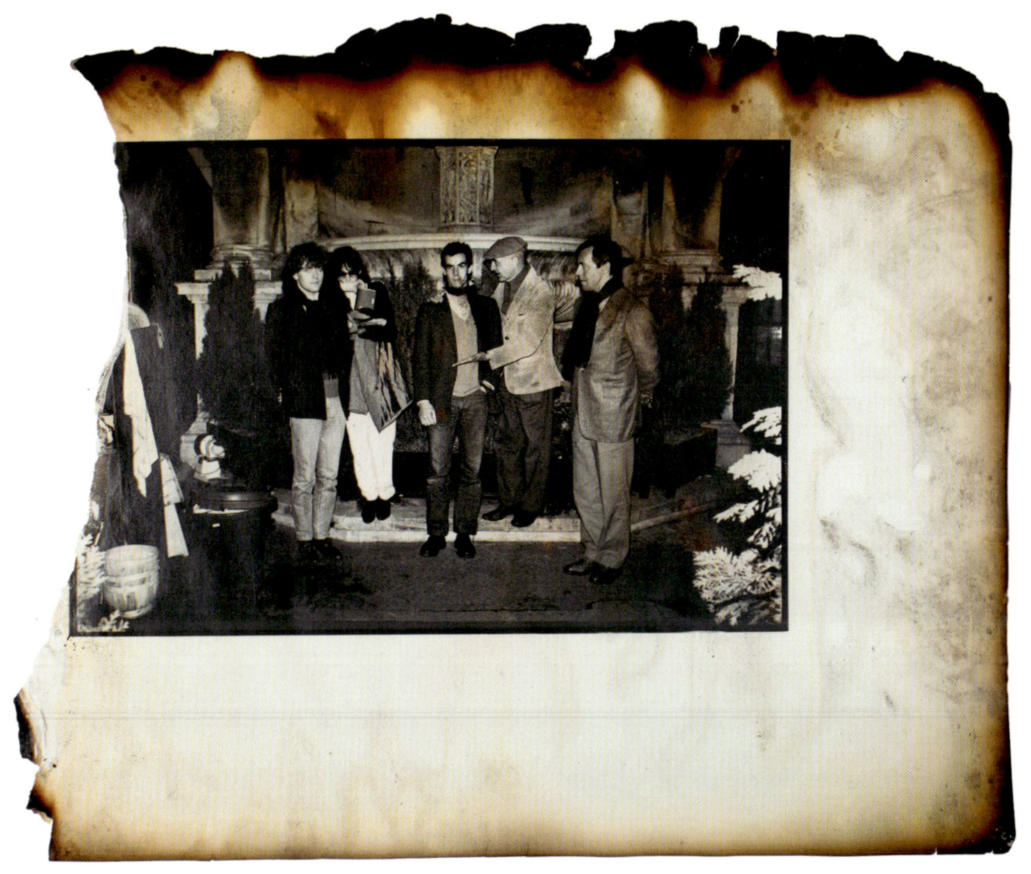

Hervé Guibert, Isabelle Adjani, Duane Michals and friends, Paris, 1981

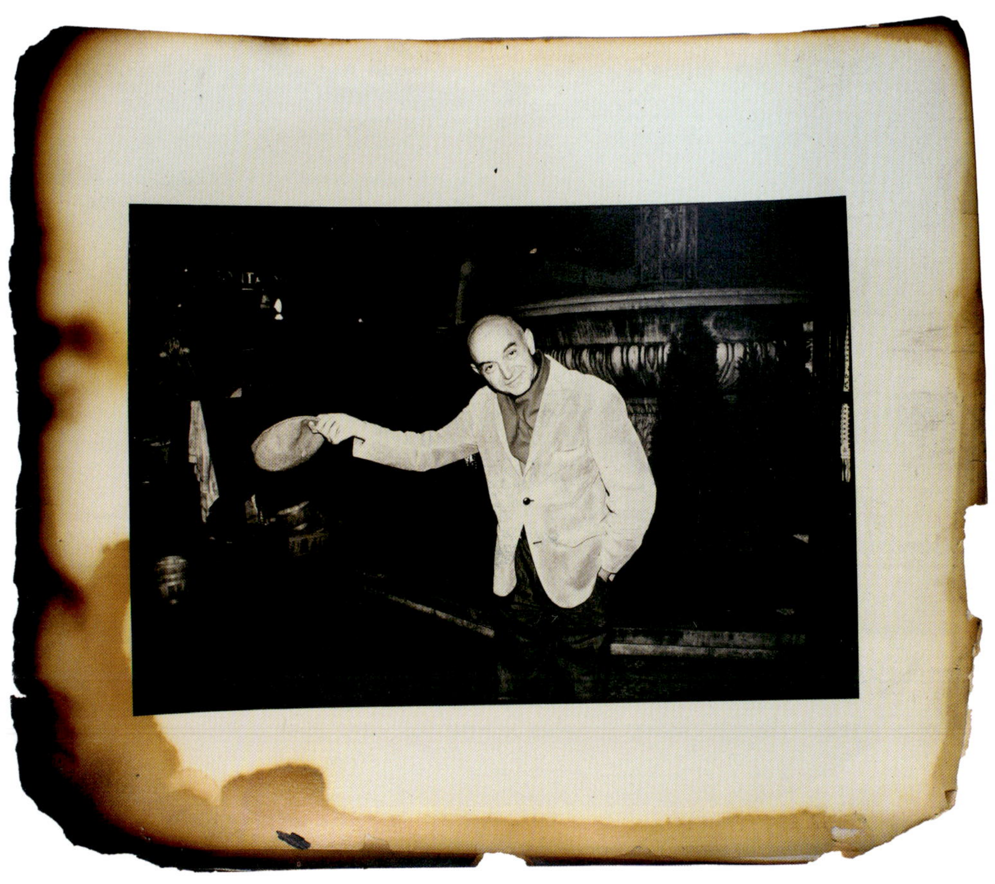

Duane Michals, Paris, 1981

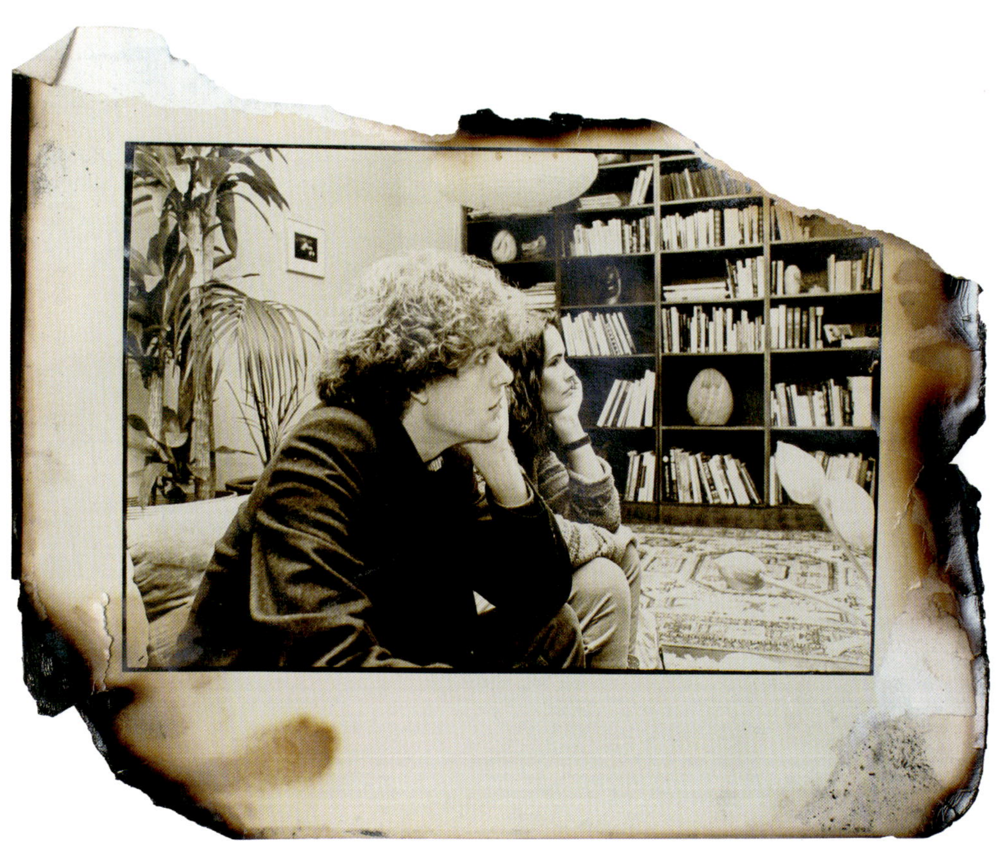

Hervé Guibert and Francine Racette, New York City, 1981

Hervé and I also did these *Le Monde* assignments together. *Le Monde* used me once a week to do a portrait for their cultural section. Until this, *Le Monde* had never run photographs in the paper. Hervé was on staff and did interviews. I think I got $50 per assignment. We profiled Jane Fonda. We had lunch with her and I took pictures of her during lunch. I didn't really get her alone for much time. We went to a very chic restaurant in the 6th but she only ate lettuce.

Who else did we profile together? In New York, in addition to Kertész, we did Donald Sutherland. We interviewed Costa-Gavras in Cannes. We did this famous antique dealer, very famous, on rue Jacob, named Madeleine Castaing. She was charming, she wore a wig held on with an elastic under her chin, it was adorable.

And then we did Orson Welles.

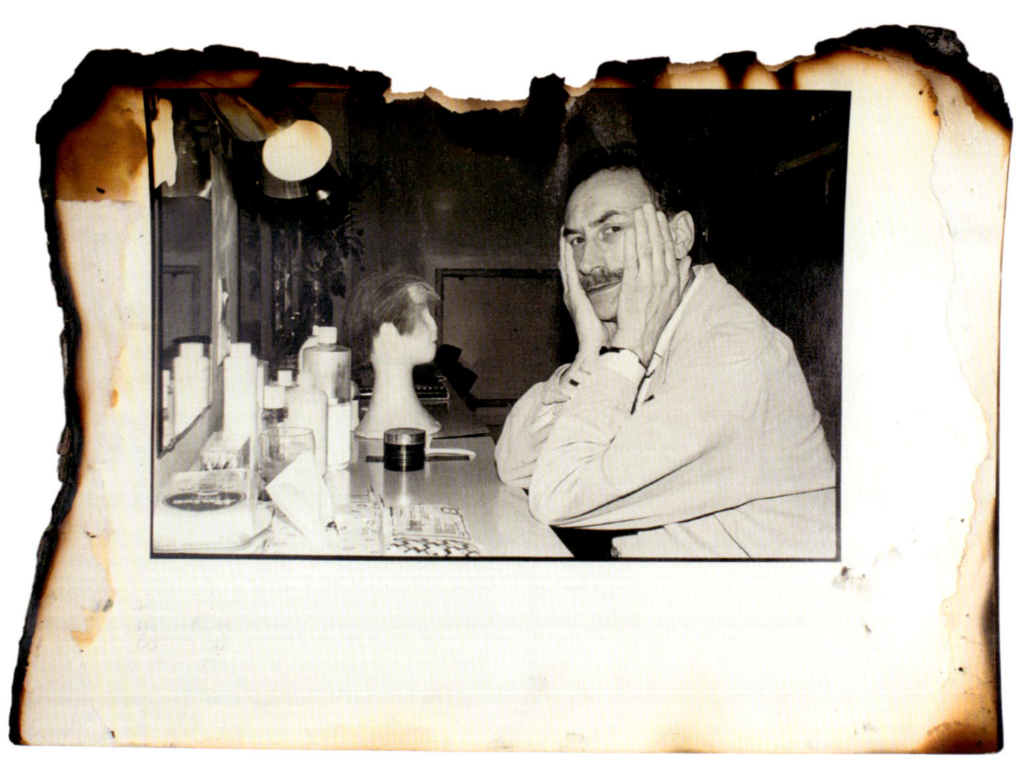

Antoine Vitez, Paris, 1982

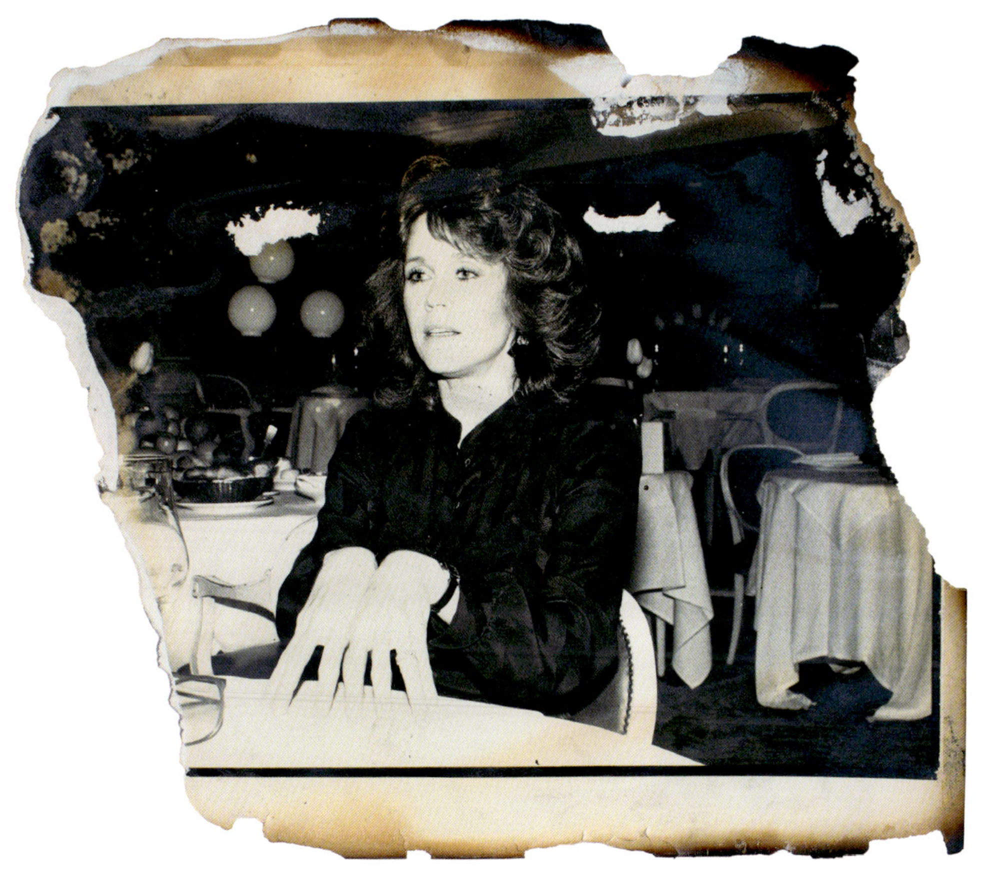

Jane Fonda, Paris, 1982

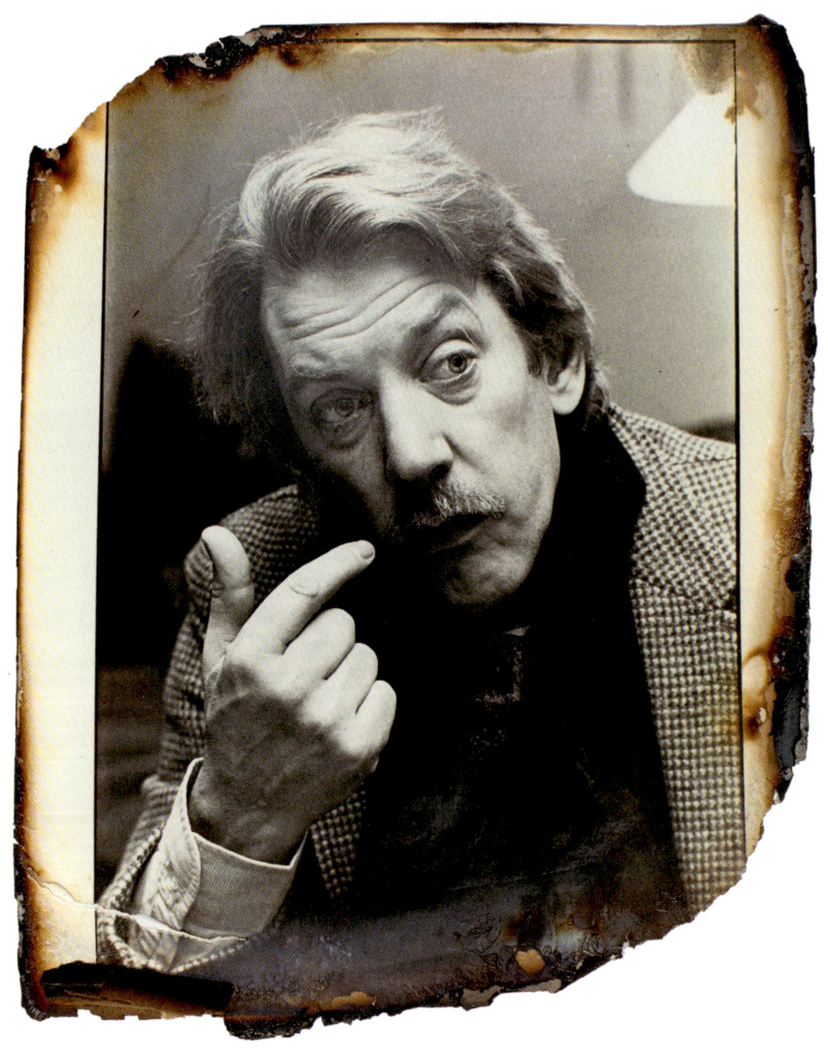

Donald Sutherland, New York City, 1981

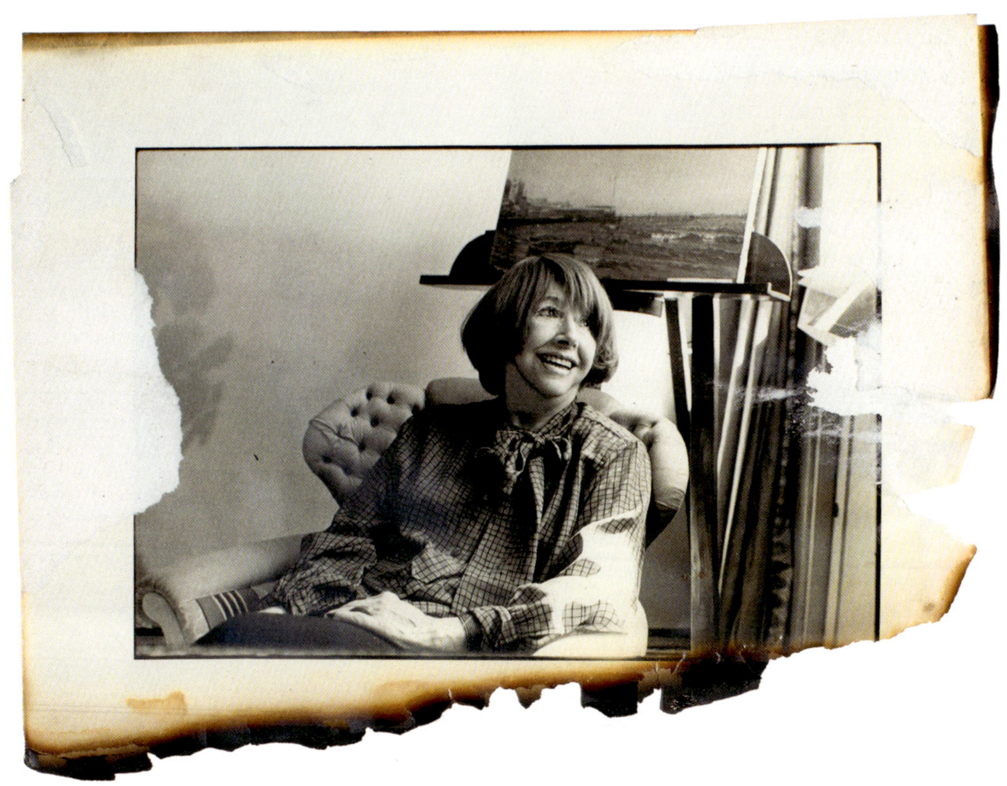

Madeleine Castaing, Paris, 1982

Orson came to Paris to receive the *Légion d'Honneur* and Hervé and I were with him for about a week. The opening sentence in Hervé's Orson piece likens him to a Bengal tiger. Orson was really not working then.

Welles was physically enormous. He had to be carried up the steps of the Palais de Chaillot to get the award from President Mitterrand. But they took him up the back steps so none of the public would see it. There was a lunch organized, and it had to be at a place where somebody had a large elevator. You know how those elevators are so teeny. It had to be at somebody's apartment where there was an elevator and the elevator had to be big enough to hold him. In this search, everybody we all knew had a walk-up. And Orson couldn't make it up the steps. So, the team from *Le Monde* found an apartment on the ground floor for this lunch.

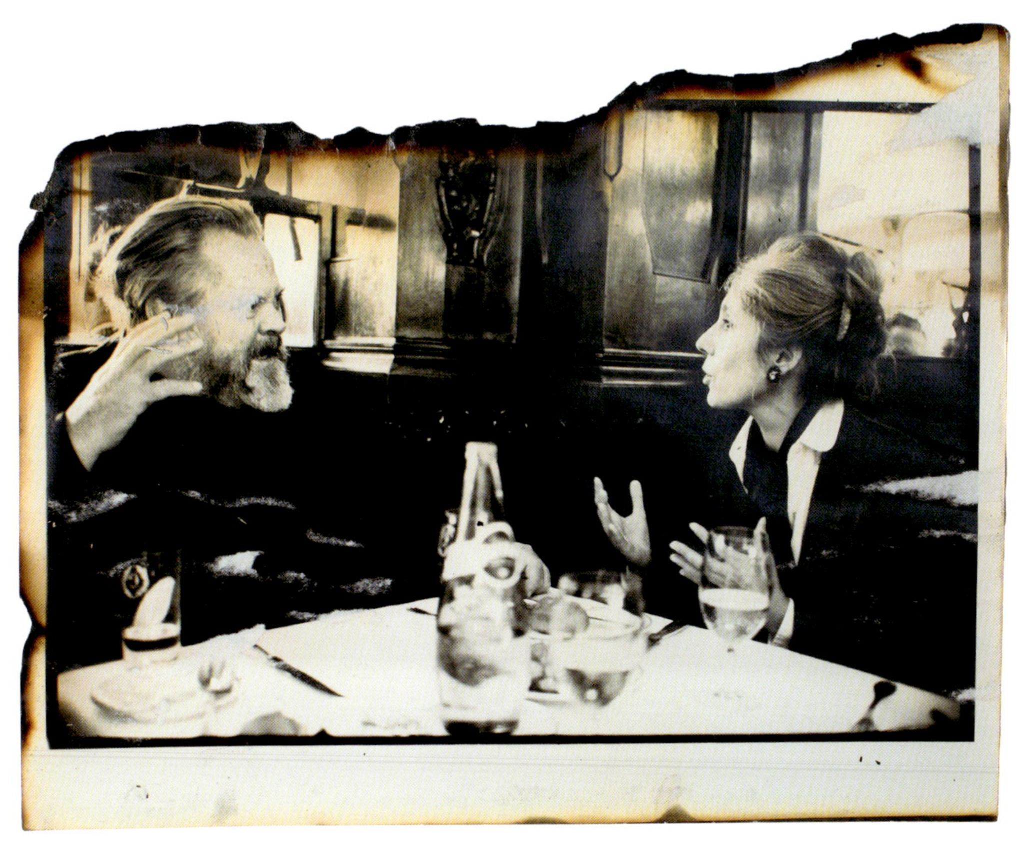

Orson Welles and Yvonne Baby, Paris, 1982

When we went to restaurants with him
he had oysters and vodka. He really
wasn't eating much, but Hervé said
that he probably went home and ate
giant steaks. He was really so big.

And he also was just so… he was just… It was like looking at, what do I want to say? He was like a caricature of a genius. His intelligence was so big and so illuminating. You don't even remember what his body is because his brain takes over the space. He was so present. That I do remember about him. He noticed and dismissed me within one split second. And I wasn't interviewing him, so it didn't matter. It is always better to be a fly on the wall.

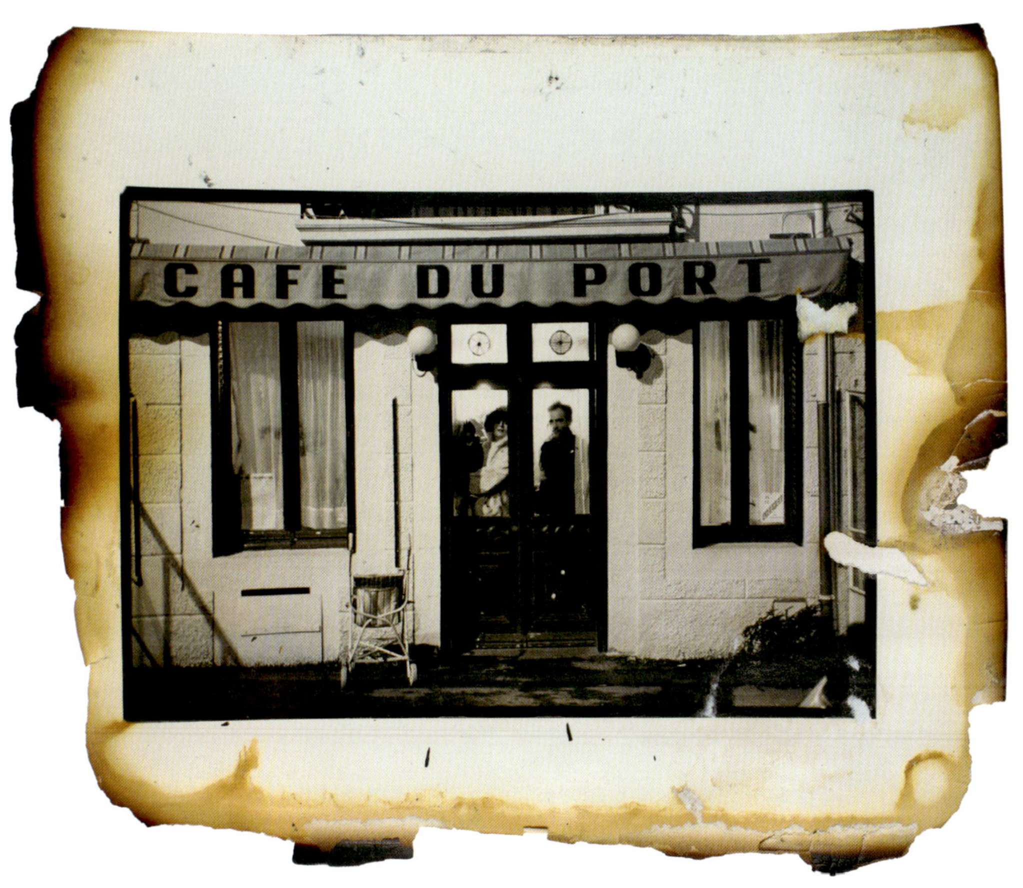

Lou, Sylvia Zerbib and Yann Babilée, Cancale, Brittany, 1984

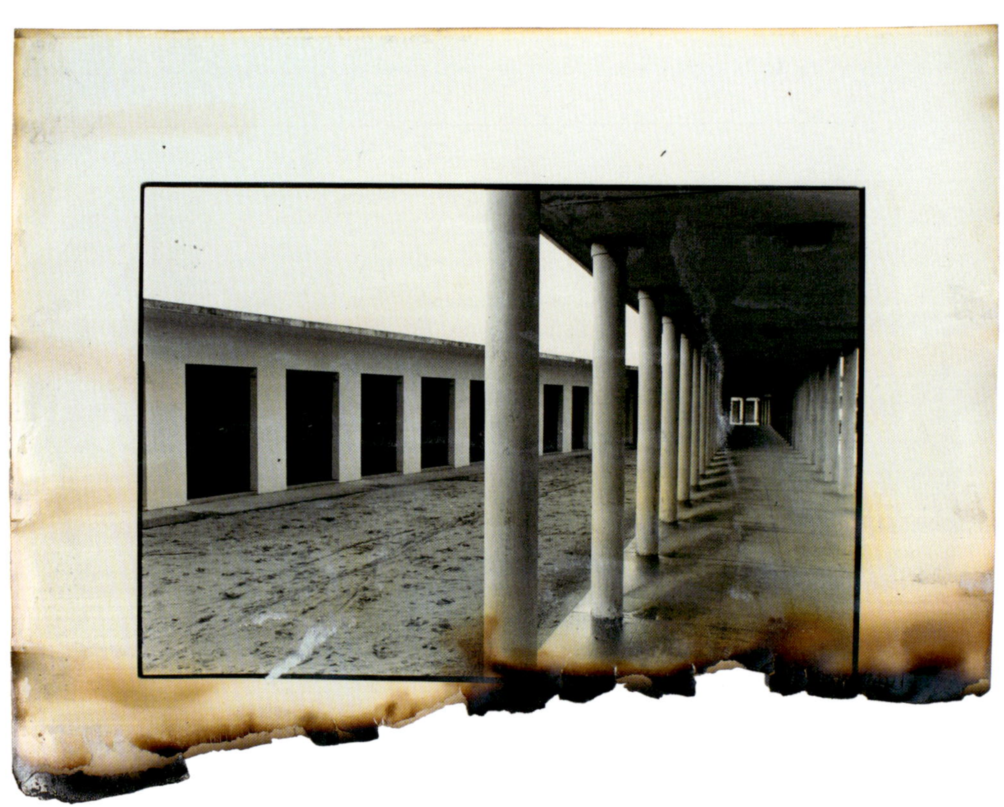

Deauville, France, 1981

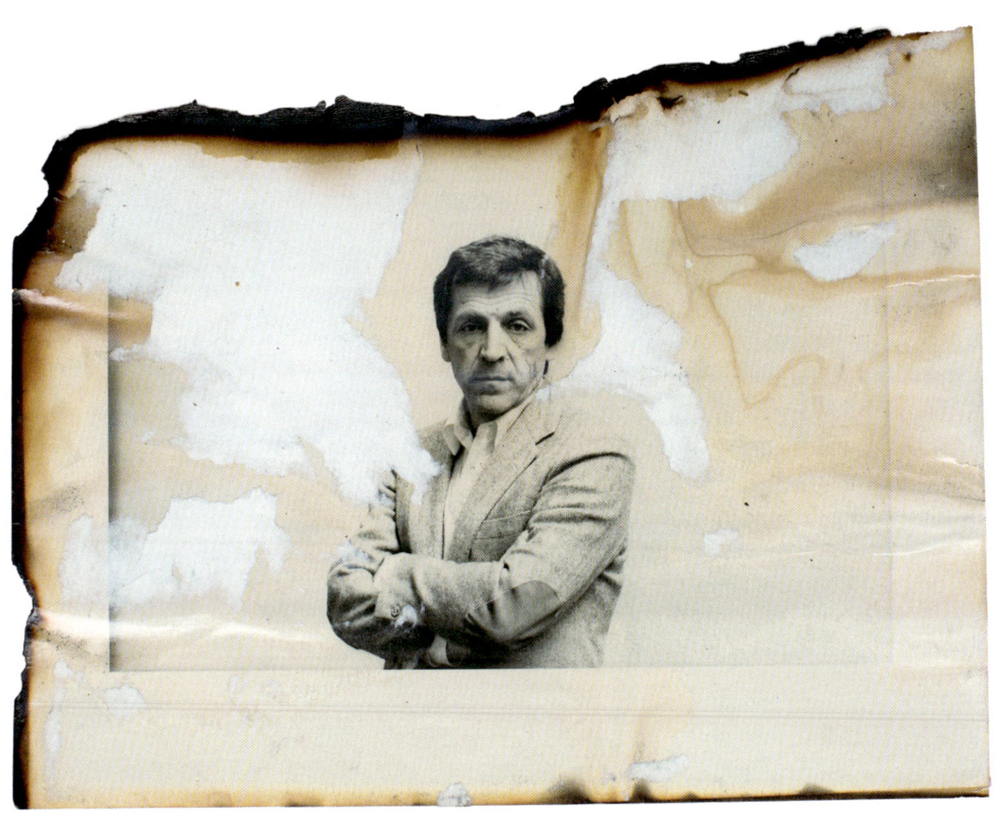

Costa-Gavras, Cannes, 1982

We really just hung out together, Hervé and I. We'd go on day trips. Take the train somewhere in the morning, walk around, take some photos, and come back at night. We went to Deauville. I'm obsessed with summer places in the winter. The beach in the winter. There's no one there, and it's a little sad, but it's also so beautiful. Ever since I was a teenager—when I became a photographer, I was like 15—we used to go to Atlantic City because it's one hour from Philadelphia. And there were horses on the beach. Unfortunately, all of those early pictures are gone, but I got totally enamored with that lonely, desolate, beachy atmosphere.

We made some beautiful, moody, dark pictures that day in Deauville, Hervé and I. He loved a portrait I did of him in front of a truck on the boardwalk and I loved one he did of me by the beach. After the fire, I found them both, damaged but beautiful. We loved the song *Tainted Love* by Soft Cell. We both had our reasons. He wanted to take me to Lourdes, but we never made it.

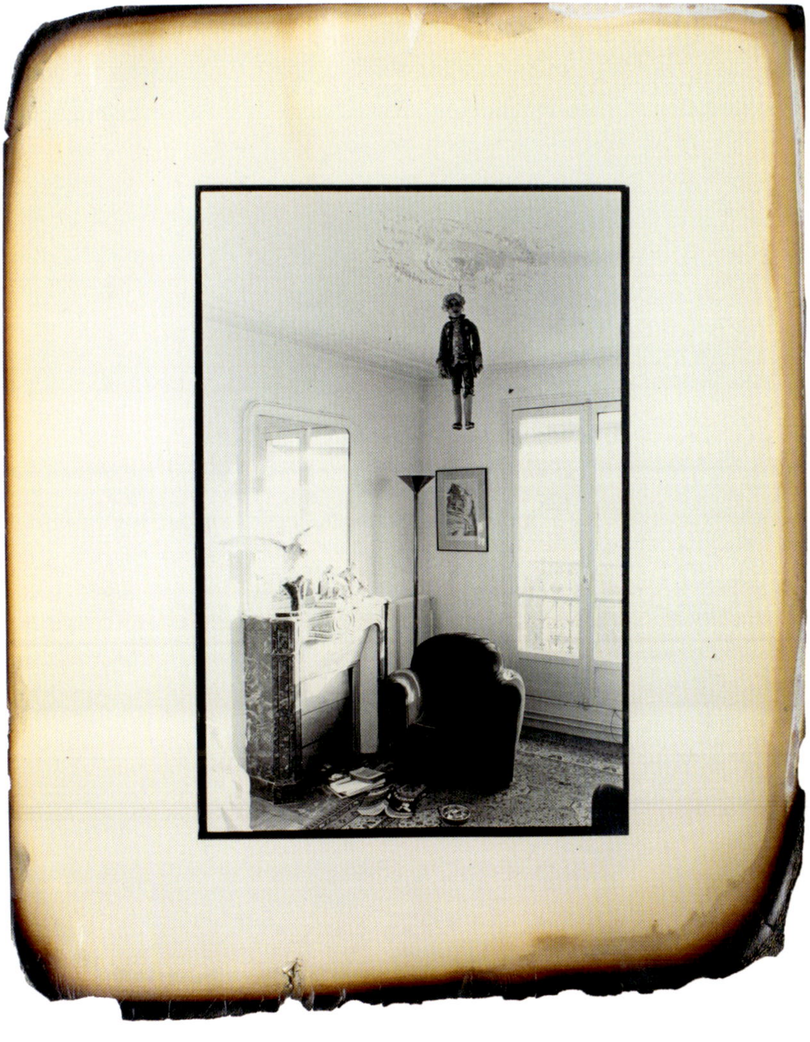

Hervé's apartment, Paris, 1982

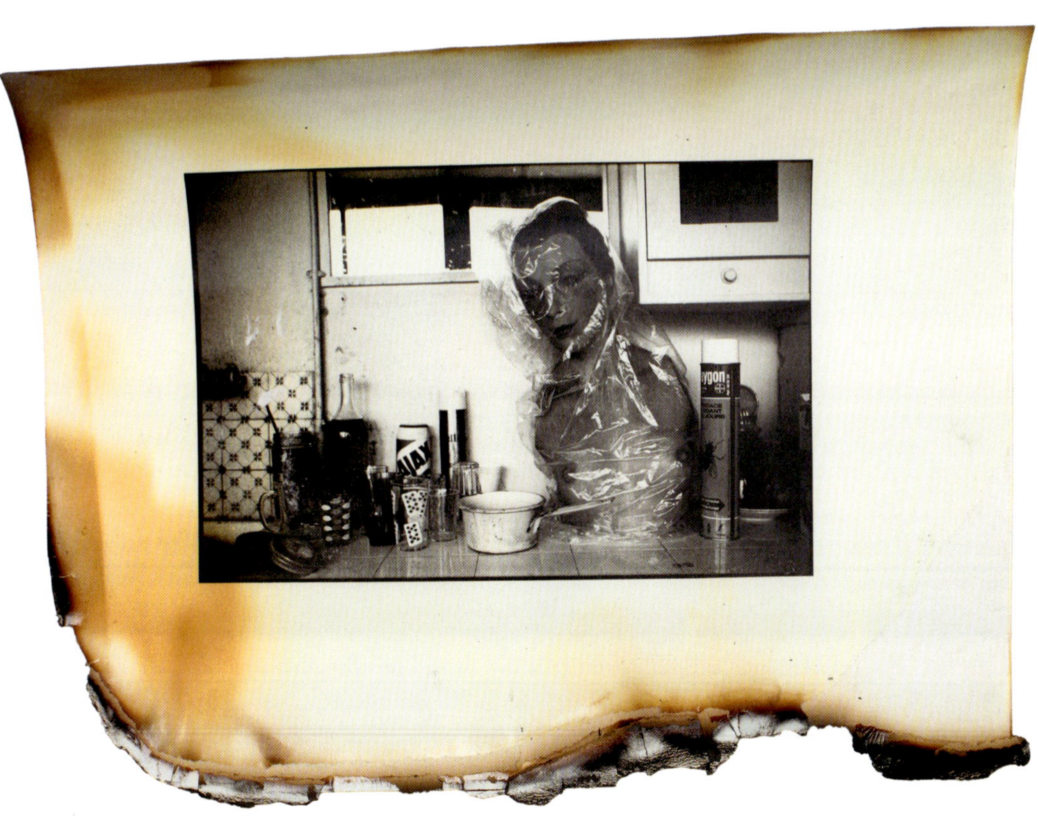

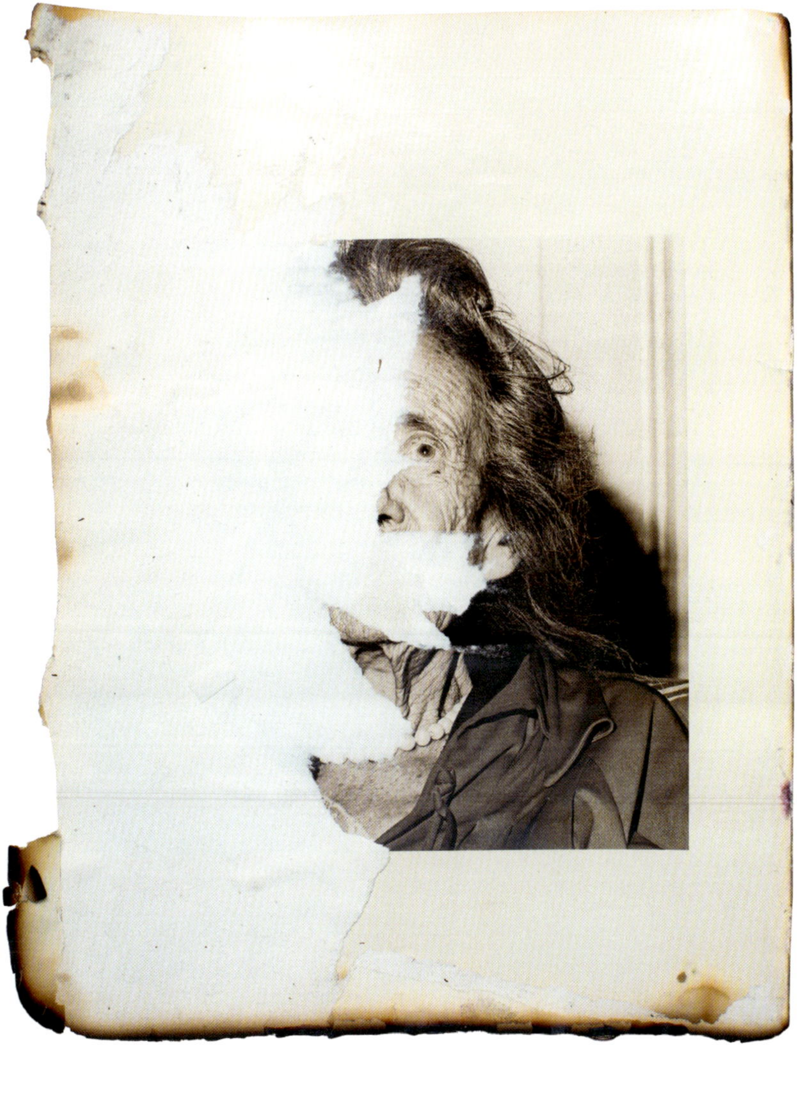

Grandma, Washington, DC, 1979

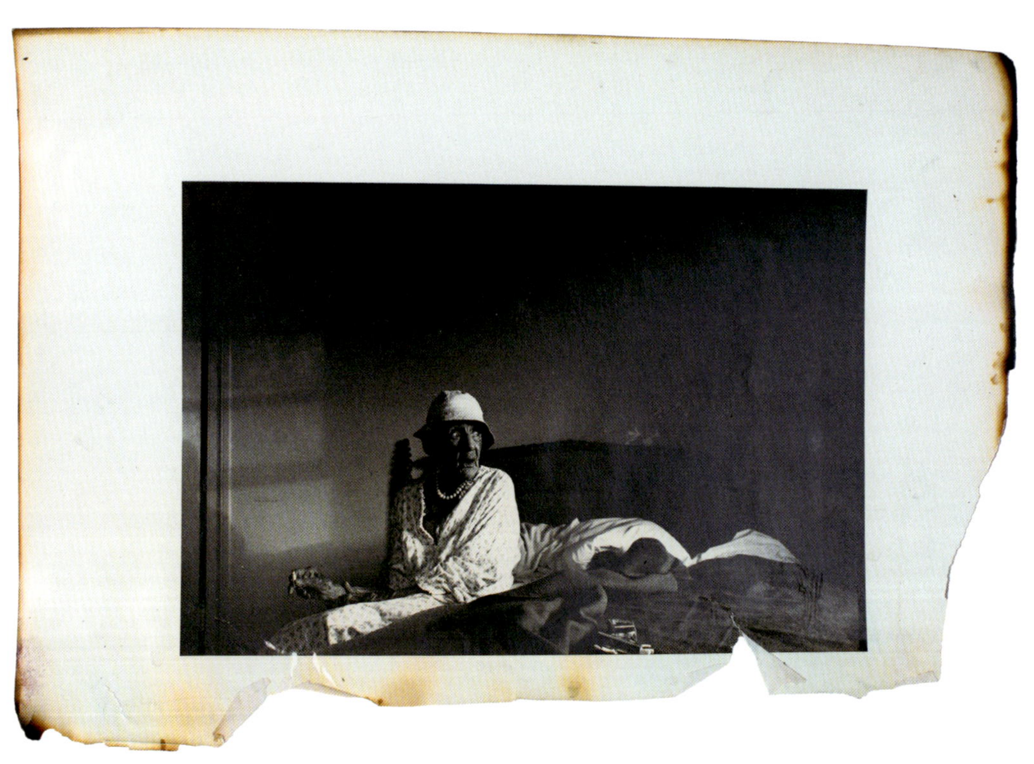

Cape May, New Jersey, 1980

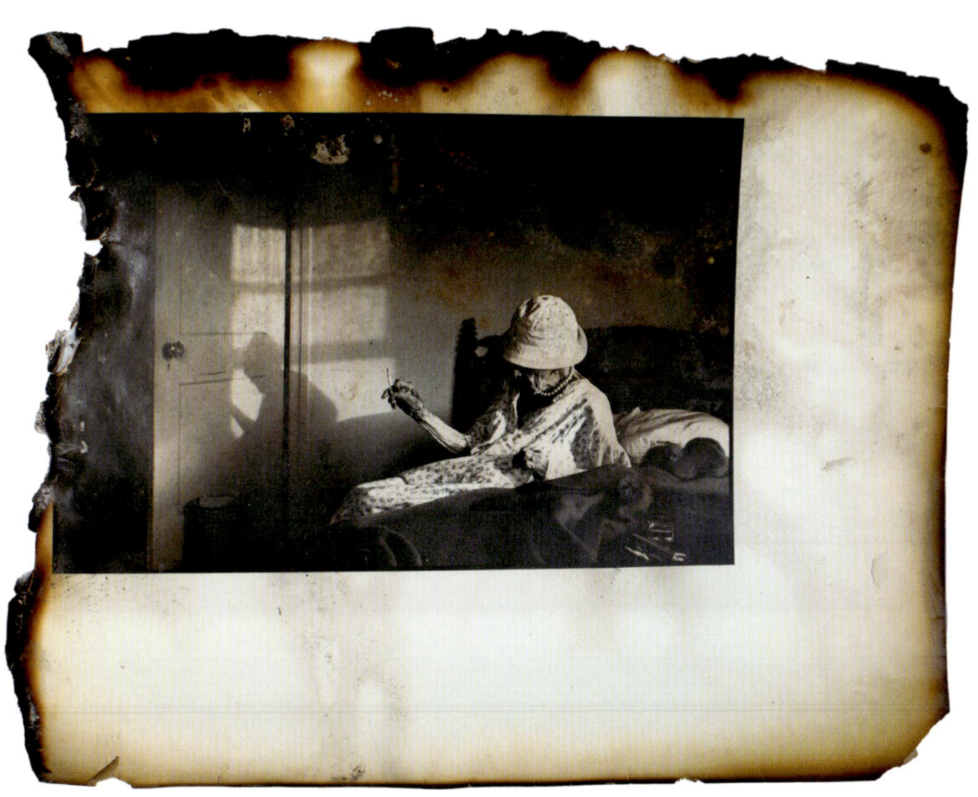

She'd say, "Why don't you take
pictures of something pretty?"

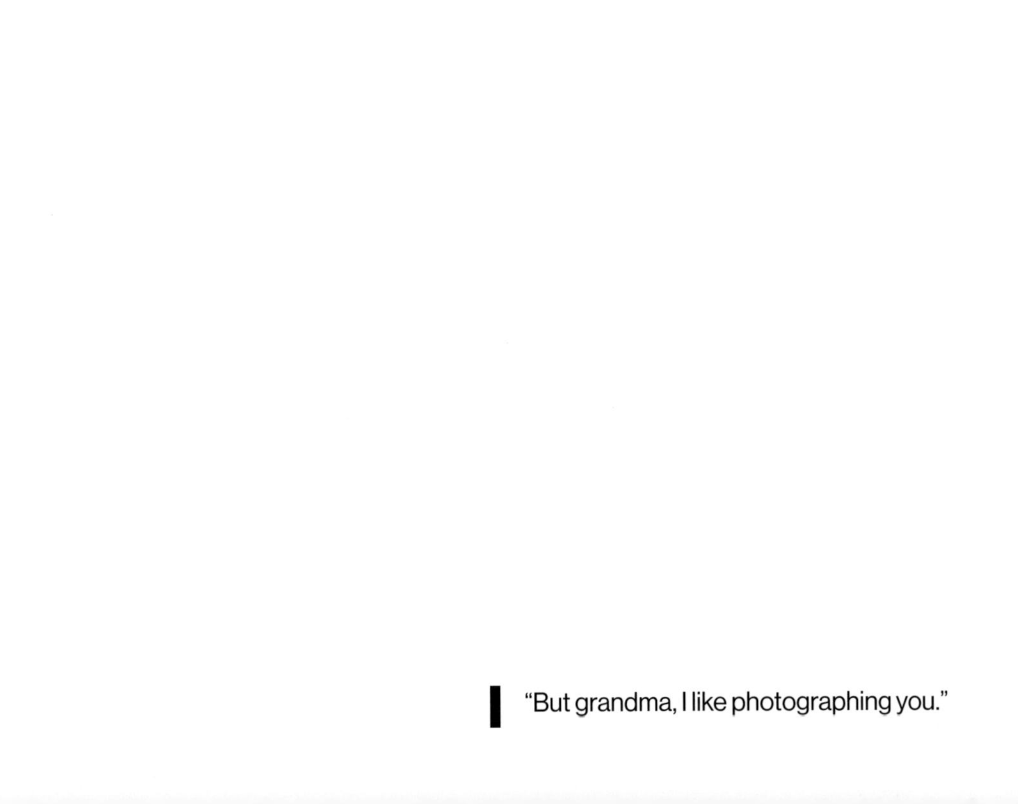
"But grandma, I like photographing you."

I said, "Grandma stop smoking!"
She said, "Leave me alone, I didn't start till I was 75."

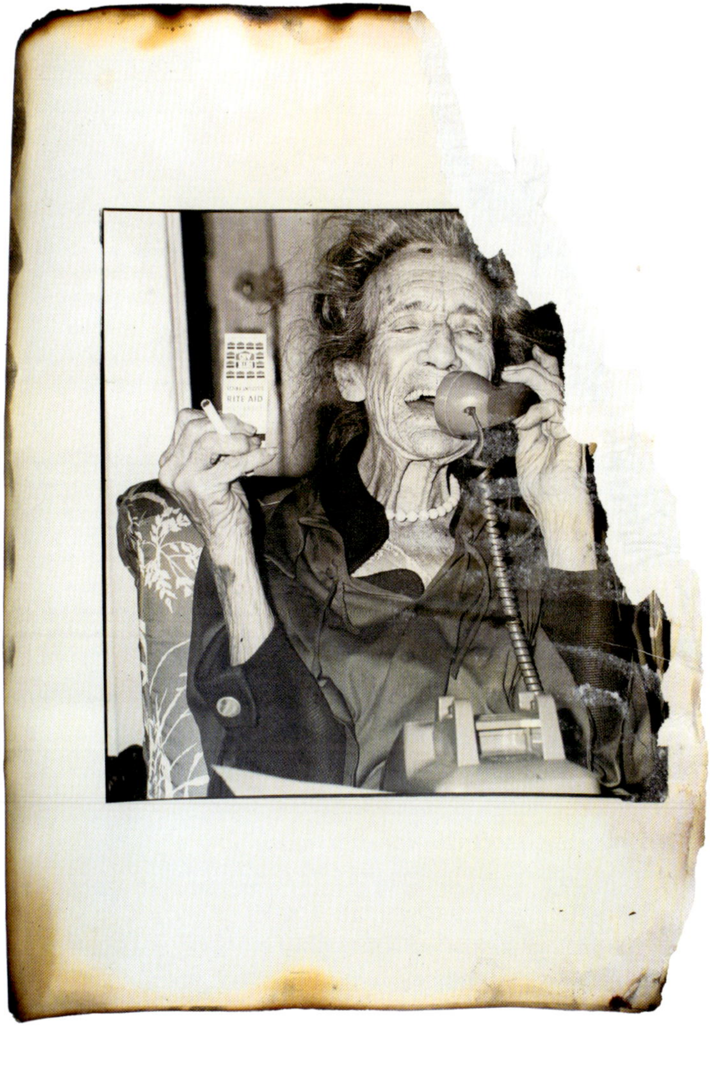

Washington, DC, 1979

Recently, I found a chandelier from her house in Georgetown. It was all boxed up. I took it out and I thought I should throw it out. Then I thought, "Nah, I'll have it cleaned." I brought it in to the guy to have it cleaned, and when I went to pick it up many months later, he said, "Man, someone really smoked a lot in that house."

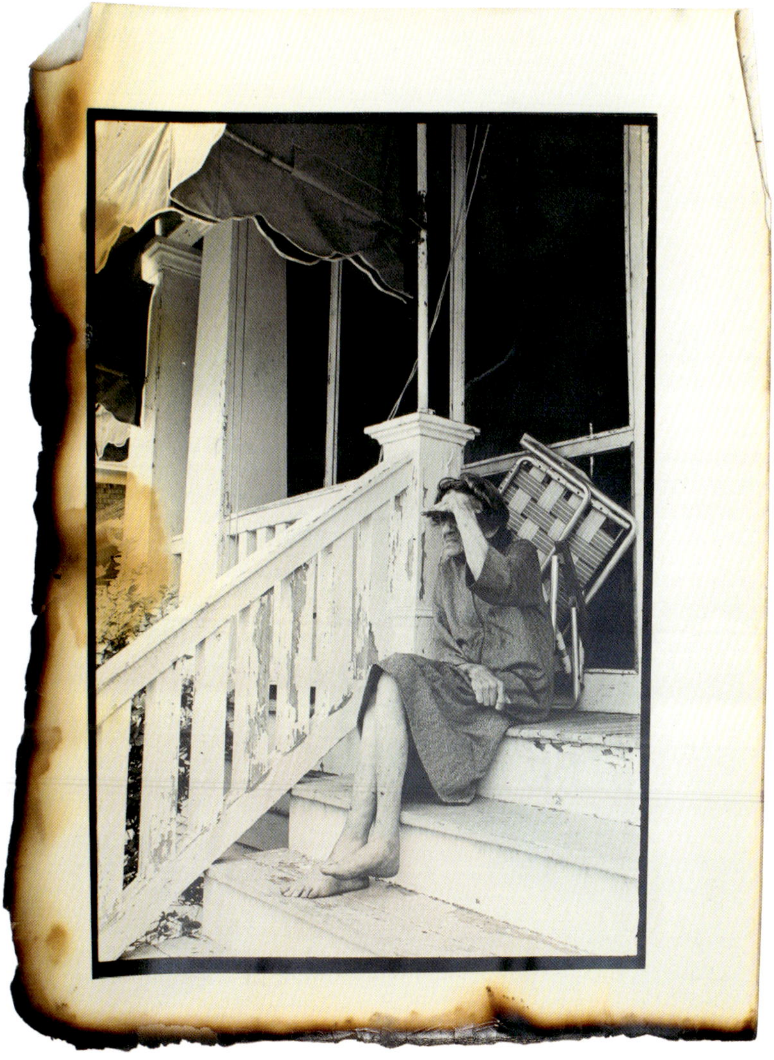

Cape May, 1979

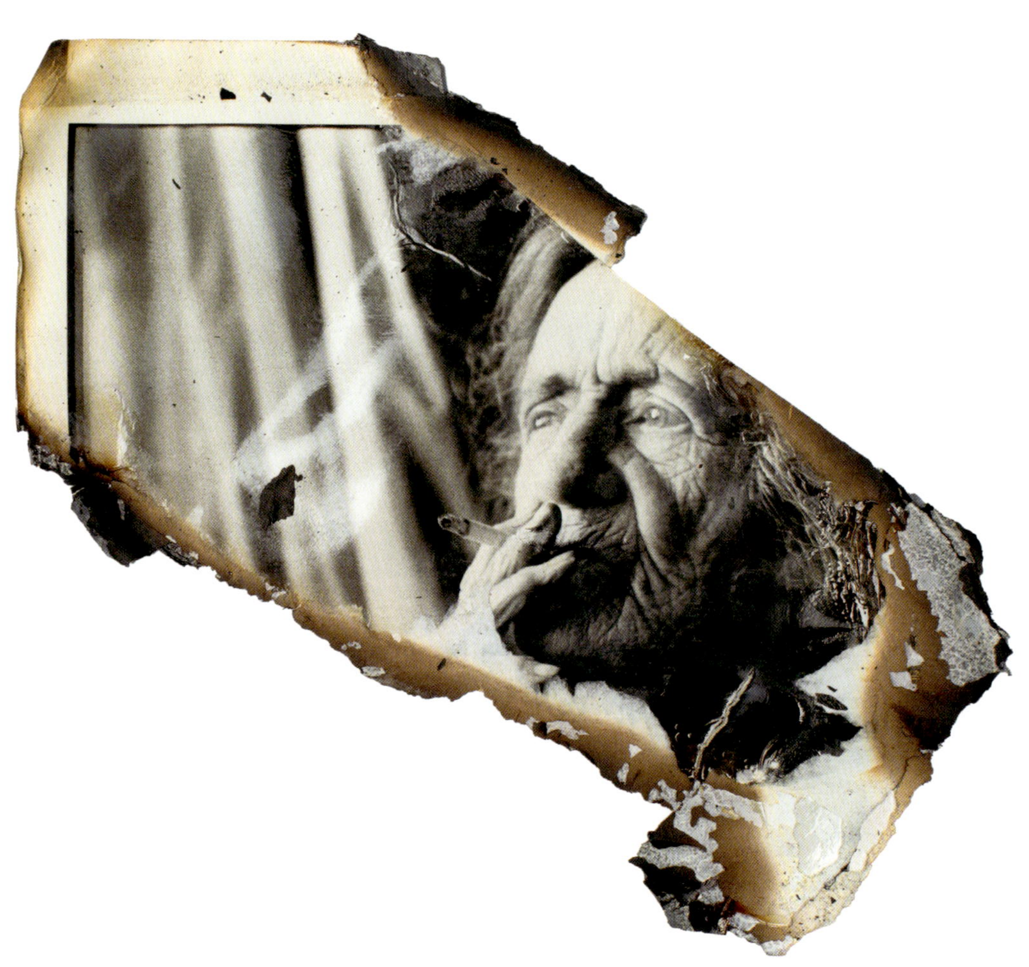

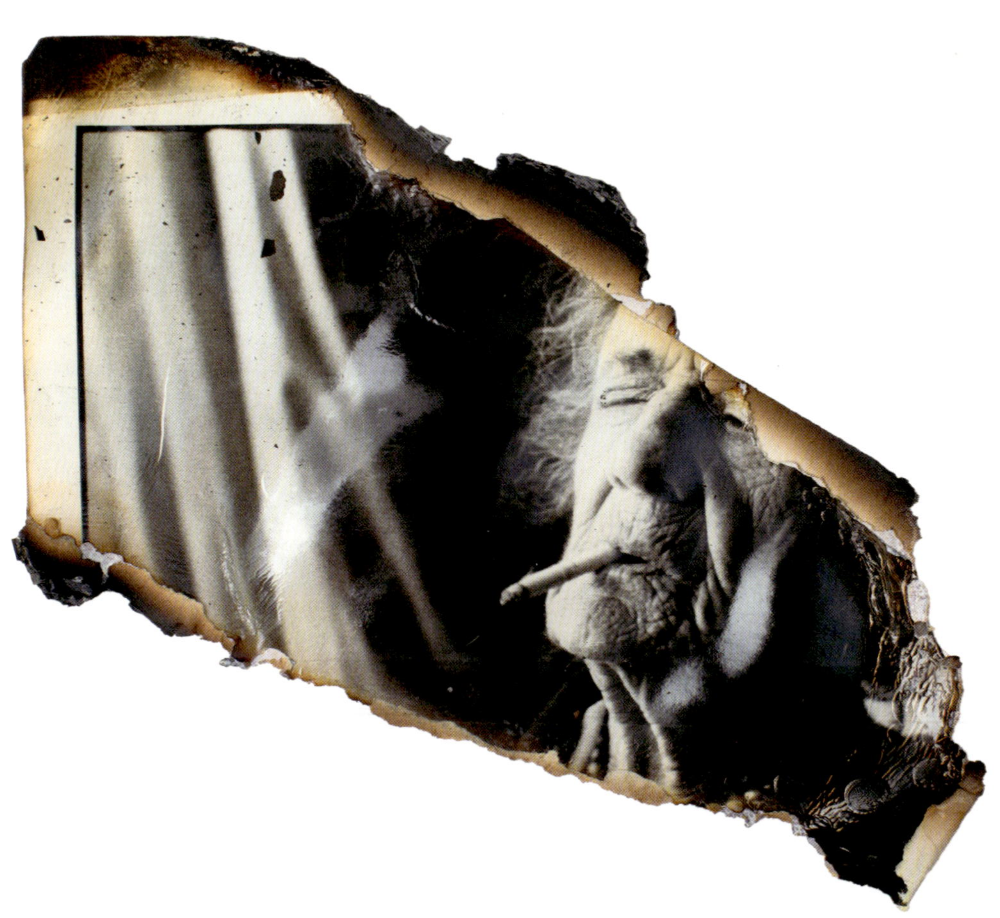

She really liked those cigs. She lived until 92, though. Never exercised. Walking seemed to be out of the question. She'd drive everywhere, a block away, even just to go to the store. She didn't have any bad habits or anything, except the cigarette thing, which, in her generation, wasn't even a neurosis. It was just what they did.

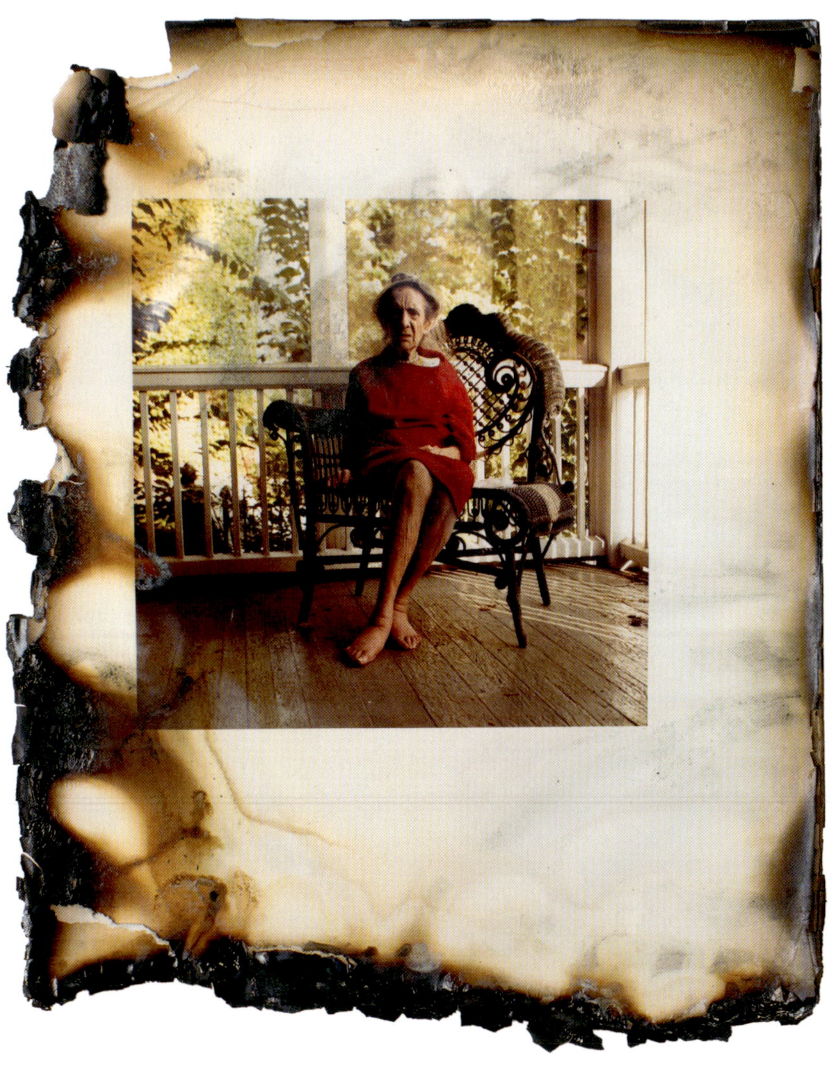

Washington, DC, 1977

I left Paris in 1983 and Hervé and I never saw
each other again.

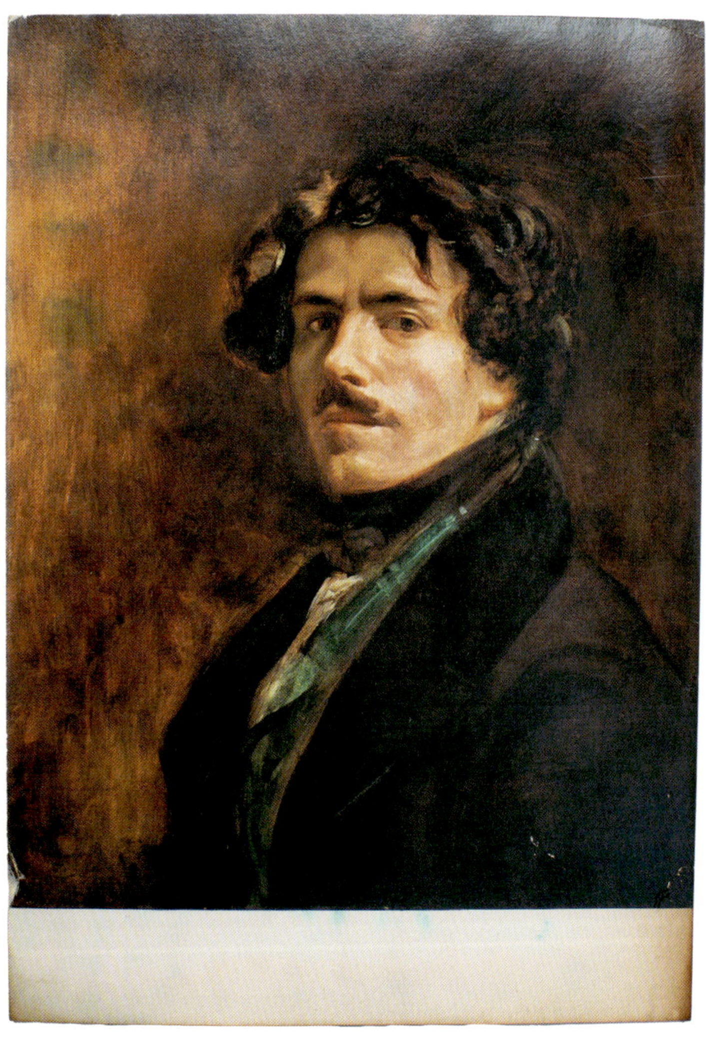

Paris le 20 avril
1983

My Dear Anne

the morning of the
afternoon of your
Haiti's postcard's
reception, alone in the
bus, I was thinking:
I'm going to write a
post-card to Anne:
"something is happening
in Paris: each day I'm
sure to see you, physically,
in the streets, but it's not
really you. A big Kiss: H.

Anne Day
2 fifth Avenue - 3N
New-York NY 10003

Amérique

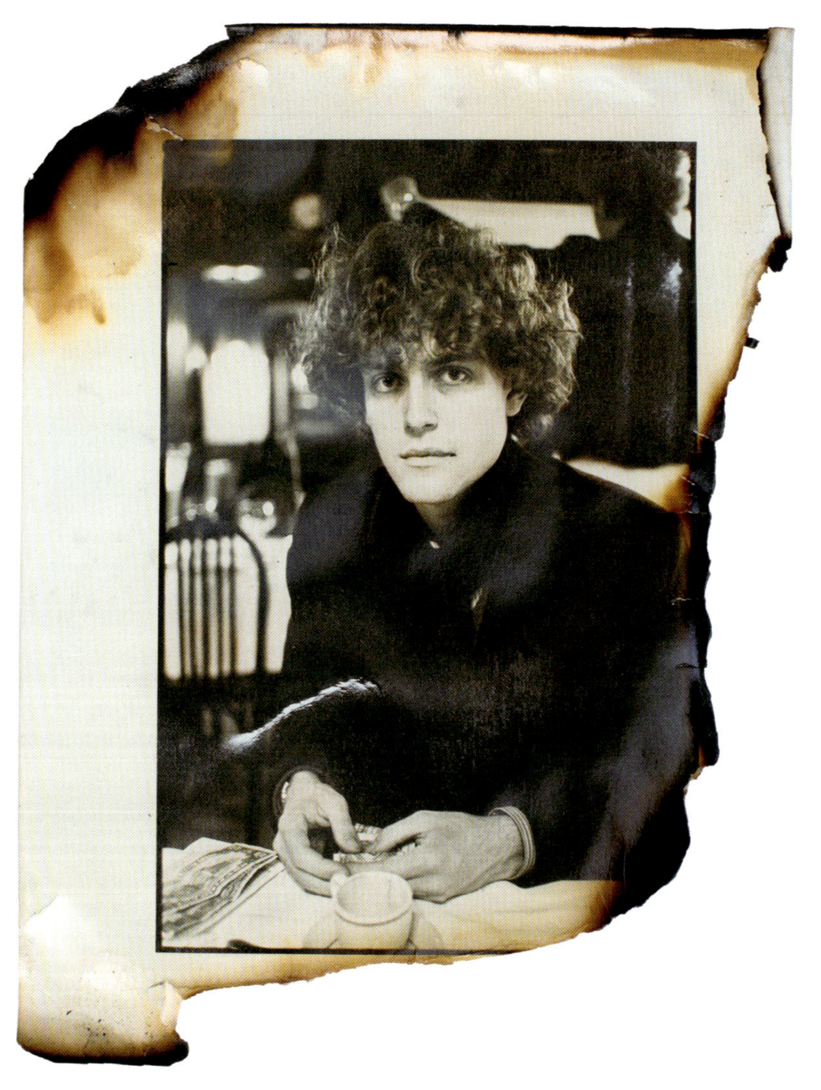

We'd send, you know, birthday cards or telegrams.
The years flew by, and then he died.

I read about it in *Time* magazine.

Years later, I was walking in New York one day and I saw a red cashmere scarf in a shop window—the exact same red that Hervé and I had always talked about.

You know, it was just one of those little games we played: 'What's the thing you want most.' A red cashmere scarf. It was a really specific red too. There was a tomato red that we didn't like, a purple red we didn't love. It was this very particular red that just seemed perfect.

ANNE DAY—day as in light—is twenty-six years old, born in Philadelphia, into a middle-class family, with many brothers and sisters. She has a beautiful face, angular and striking, dark eyes, and great love for a ninety-five year old grandmother who took up smoking at the age of seventy-five. She photographs her, in bed, or almost everywhere, grumbling or bursting into laughter, but never has her pose. She has been photographing her for ten years and hopes one day to make a book of these photos. Anne became a photographer after studying painting, feeling she lacked the talent for painting for the medium.

Anne is a freelance photographer, always waiting for a phone call, a commission, a cocktail party or a political rally in Chicago, shots for a tabloid, small gigs.

Anne prints her own photos, has set up a darkroom in a cupboard and locks herself in at nightfall with her telephone and radio, amidst the slightly acrid odour of chemicals, and sometimes remains there until 6 a.m., because she doesn't like being locked up in the dark while others are out bustling around in the daylight.

Like many photographers, forced to do any job that comes along to pay the rent, Anne complains that she no longer has time for her own work. A publisher has asked her to shoot the photos, black-and-white and colour, for a book on the Library of Congress in Washington, a painstaking and humbling job that involves reproducing architectural detail and painted friezes as faithfully as possible.

Anne takes advantage of her time in Washington to visit her grandmother, who lives in the area. Over time, and in retrospect, her professional work could well become her personal work—her flash photos of cocktail parties are no worse than those of Larry Fink or Tod Papageorge, and her architectural photos have an astonishing graphic quality.

—Hervé Guibert
Le Monde
Published March 26, 1981

LES FLASHS D'ANNE
Anne Day

Edited by Jordan Weitzman

© 2025 Anne Day for the images and text
© 2025 Magic Hour Press for this edition

"Les Flashs D'Anne" *Le Monde* article
translated by Alison Strayer.
Author photos by Hervé Guibert courtesy
of Christine Guibert.

Book design by Jordan Weitzman
Typeset by Jason Fulford
Proofread by Charity Coleman
Pre-press by Heyward Hart
Printed in Italy at EBS

Distributed by
ARTBOOK/DAP
75 Broad Street, Suite 630
New York, NY 10004
Artbook.com

ISBN 978-1-7389013-5-7

www.magichour.press

Thank you Roger and Yvonne for introducing me to Hervé, Charmaine for introducing me to Elizabeth and Elizabeth for introducing me to Jordan. Thank you to Sylvia Zerbib for her long, unwavering friendship. Thank you to all of the friends who helped me resuscitate these precious images.

—Anne Day

The publisher would like to thank Elizabeth Gaffin, without whom this book would not exist. Thank you also Noah Britton, Gabriel Cholette, Moyra Davey, Jason Fulford, Christine Guibert, and Francis Schichtel.

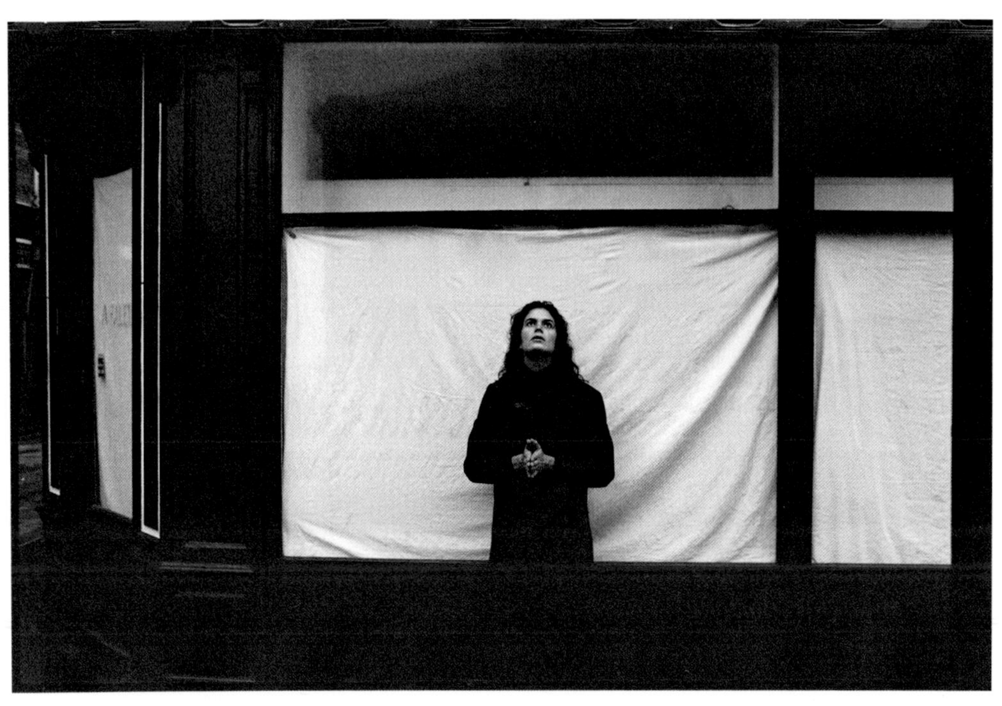

Anne Day, Paris, by Hervé Guibert, 1982

Photos à New-York

Les flashs d'Anne

ANNE DAY, day comme le jour, a vingt-six ans, née à Philadelphie, de parents bourgeois moyens, beaucoup de frères et sœurs, un beau visage carré, bien dessiné, des yeux sombres, et l'amour pour une grand-mère de quatre-vingt-quinze ans qui s'est mise à fumer à l'âge de soixante-quinze ans. Elle la photographie, au lit, partout, en train de râler, ou dans un grand rire soudain, elle ne la fait jamais poser. Elle la photographie depuis dix ans et espère faire un jour un livre de ces photos. Anne est devenue photographe, après des études de peinture, parce qu'elle ne se sentait pas assez douée pour la peinture.

Anne est photographe free-lance, toujours en attente d'un coup de fil, d'une commande, une coktail-party ou un meeting de politiciens à Chicago, des snap-shots pour un journal de potins, des petites factures. Anne tire elle-même ses photos, elle a installé une chambre noire dans un placard, et elle s'y enferme, dans l'odeur un peu âcre des bains chimiques, à la tombée de la nuit, avec son téléphone et son poste de radio, jusqu'à 6 heures du matin parfois, car elle n'aime pas être ainsi enfermée, dans le noir quand les autres s'activent dans la lumière.

Comme beaucoup de photographes, qui sont forcés d'accepter tout et n'importe quoi pour vivre, Anne se plaint de ne plus avoir le temps de travailler pour elle. Un éditeur lui a demandé de réaliser les photos, en noir et blanc et en couleur, pour un livre sur la Library of Congress à Washington, un travail laborieux et humble qui consiste à reproduire, le plus piqué possible, le plus fidèlement possible, des détails d'architecture, de frises peintes.

Mais Anne profite de ses séjours à Washington pour retrouver sa grand-mère, qui vit dans les environs. Son travail professionnel pourrait un jour devenir son travail personnel, avec la bonification du temps, et avec le recul : ses photos au flash des coktail-parties ne sont pas moins bonnes que celles de Larry Fink ou de Tod Papageorge, et ses photos d'architecture ont une qualité graphique étonnante.

Hugh Crawford, qui n'est pas le petit-fils de Joan, a le même âge qu'Anne, lui aussi photographe. Timide et se rattachant facilement à la théorie, l'affectant même, pour aborder la photo, ce grand admirateur de Meyerowitz montre un travail impeccable, en couleur, format 6 × 6, des portraits de visages ingrats, qui rappellent parfois ceux que choisissait Arbus, et surtout les couleurs clinquantes, flashées en plein jour, des manèges de fêtes foraines ou des stations-service désertes. On pense aux nuits d'Ollman. Mais dans le travail en noir et blanc, plus secret, plus tâtonnant, peut se cacher, déjà, une photo superbe, comme cette jeune fille en décapotable, les cheveux au vent, mais dont l'arrière-plan laisse émerger, comme de son imagination, une maison fantôme...

EN 1940, à New-York, dans les quartiers pauvres, à Harlem, dans la banlieue de Brooklyn, les enfants sont dans la rue. Ils jouent avec trois fois rien, masqués d'un morceau de papier, ils deviennent des gentlemen louches, puis ils se transforment en gangsters et en flics, ils se tuent, ils s'embrassent, ils se contorsionnent, ils se dénudent pour se doucher sous les geysers des lances à incendie, puisqu'une nouvelle loi le leur permet ils grimpent aux arbres comme de petits singes accrochés à la vie, ils inventent tous les drames, ils caricaturent les actions des adultes, et une femme est là pour les regarder, à distance, et pour capturer leur génie inconscient.

En 1940, Helen Levitt a vingt-deux ans. Elle vient de découvrir la photo, à travers une exposition de Cartier-Bresson, qu'elle n'a pas encore rencontré. « Mon inspiration a été Henri, raconte-t-elle. J'ai vu quelques-unes de ses photographies, dans les années 30, dans des galeries, ici et là, je ne me souviens pas où. A l'époque, je n'avais pas d'ambitions particulières, je venais d'une famille pauvre de la banlieue de Brooklyn, j'avais arrêté mes études, j'étais une « drop out ». D'abord, je n'ai pas compris ce que je regardais, mais j'ai réalisé l'infini des possibilités. Ses photos m'ont révélé un moyen d'être en vie. Je devais trouver mon propre chemin.

» J'ai commencé à travailler dans les quartiers pauvres, parce que là les gens vivaient leur vie dans la rue. Dans les quartiers riches, ils s'enferment dans les étages. Et, dans les quartiers d'affaires, ils courent trop vite. Je n'étais pas bonne pour le mouvement, j'étais meilleure pour les choses établies. Je m'asseyais sur les escaliers, je marchais beaucoup, seule, il y avait beaucoup à voir et beaucoup à photographier. Je n'avais pas de relations avec les gens, je restais à distance et je m'évanouissais dès que la photo était prise, vous savez comment travaille Henri.

» Depuis, New-York a beaucoup changé. Dans les années 40, les gens ne voyaient pas l'appareil photo. Maintenant tout le monde est conscient, tout le monde possède un appareil, et c'est très difficile ch...

To make money

Ni Anne Day ni Hugh Crawford ne sont exposés dans les galeries new-yorkaises, ils ont bien dû, sans doute, un jour ou l'autre, y présenter leur travail, et ils devront y retourner plusieurs fois avant qu'une porte s'ouvre vraiment. Le marché américain de la photographie laisse rarement une chance aux jeunes photographes inconnus : on [...] William Klein après [...] èglement, et [...] lleristes » [...] auprès [...] ou [...]

petits morceaux de vie ou d'espace suspendus pouvaient former un capital, être l'objet de transactions, de convoitises, de vols, d'expertises, bientôt de faux. La photographie est une matière comme une autre, et pourquoi échapperait-elle à la loi de l'argent ? La photographie aux Etats-Unis pour le Français profane qui ne fait qu'en recevoir des échantillons, par l'intermédiaire des magazines, représente le sommet, le ad hoc, le nec plus ultra, l'aboutissement pour l'Européen, la consécration, le modèle.

On vous demande ici : « Est-ce que ça marche la photo en France ? », et on vous répond : « Ça commence, ça commence, oh, ce n'est pas encore l'Amérique, mais on va bien y arriver, [...] Or [...]